Unraveling Denim

Special Issue edited by
Sophie Woodward and
Daniel Miller

Textile

EDITED BY
CATHERINE HARPER
AND DORAN ROSS

THE JOURNAL OF
CLOTH AND CULTURE

VOLUME 9
ISSUE 1
MARCH 2011

ORDERING INFORMATION

Three Issues per volume. One volume per annum.
2011: Volume 9
ONLINE
www.bergpublishers.com
BY MAIL
Berg Publishers
C/O Turpin Distribution Services
Pegasus Drive
Stratton Business Park
Biggleswade
Bedfordshire SG18 8TQ
UK
BY FAX
+ 44 (0)1767 601640
BY TELEPHONE
+ 44 (0)1767 604951
For Subscription Enquiries
email custserv@turpin-distribution.com
ENQUIRIES
Editorial: Julia Hall
email jhall@bergpublishers.com
Production: Ken Bruce
email kbruce@bergpbublishers.com
Advertising: Ellie Graves
email egraves@bergpublishers.com
SUBSCRIPTION RATES
Institutional
Print and online: 1 year: £170/US$331; 2 year: £272/US$530
Online only: 1 year: £144/US$282; 2 year: £231/US$451
Individual
Print: 1 year: £49/US$85; 2 year: £78/US$136
Full color images available online
Access your electronic subscription through
www.ingentaconnect.com
Berg Publishers is the imprint of
Oxford International Publishers Ltd.

EDITORS

Catherine Harper
University of Brighton, UK
Doran Ross
Fowler Museum at UCLA
Founding Editor and Associate Editor:
Pennina Barnett, Goldsmiths, University of London, UK
p.barnett@gold.ac.uk
Founding Editor and Associate Editor:
Janis Jefferies, Goldsmiths, University of London, UK
j.jefferies@gold.ac.uk
Associate Editor:
Mary Littrell, Colorado State University
mlittrel@cah.colostate.edu
Editorial Assistant:
Sara Duffy
textileculture@brighton.ac.uk
Book Reviews Editor:
Victoria Mitchell, Norwich School of Art & Design,
St George Street, Norwich NR3 1BB, UK
v.mitchell@nsad.ac.uk
Exhibition Reviews Editors:
UK and Rest of World
Deborah Southerland, Faculty of Creative Arts, University of the
West of England, Bower Ashton Campus, Kennel Lodge Road,
Bristol BS3 2JT, UK
Deborah.Southerland@uwe.ac.uk
USA
Geraldine Ondrizek, Art Department Chair, Reed College,
Portland, OR 97202, USA
ondrizeg@reed.edu
Rebecca Stevens, Contemporary Textiles, The Textile Museum,
23250 S Street NW, Washington, DC 20008-4088, USA
stevensgrj@aol.com

AIMS AND SCOPE

Cloth accesses an astonishingly broad range of human experiences. The raw material from which things are made, it has various associations: sensual, somatic, decorative, functional and ritual. Yet although textiles are part of our everyday lives, their very familiarity and accessibility belie a complex set of histories, and invite a range of speculations about their personal, social and cultural meanings. This ability to move within and reference multiple sites gives textiles their potency.

This journal brings together research in textiles in an innovative and distinctive academic forum for all those who share a multifaceted view of textiles within an expanded feld. Representing a dynamic and wide-ranging set of critical practices, it provides a platform for points of departure between art and craft; gender and identity; cloth, body and architecture; labor and technology; techno-design and practice—all situated within the broader contexts of material and visual culture.

Textile invites submissions informed by technology and visual media, history and cultural theory; anthropology; philosophy; political economy and psychoanalysis. It draws on a range of artistic practices, studio and digital work, manufacture and object production.

Berg Publishers is a member of CrossRef

INTERNATIONAL ADVISORY BOARD

Ingrid Bachmann
Concordia University, Canada

Elizabeth Barber
Occidental College, USA

Dilys Blum
Philadelphia Museum of Art, USA

Grace Cochrane
Independent Curator and Writer, Australia

Susan Conway
Parson's School of Design, USA, and the British Museum, UK

Jasleen Dhamija
Independent Scholar/Consultant, India

Linda Eaton
Winterthur Museum, USA

Joan Farrer
University of Brighton, UK

Jennifer Harris
The Whitworth Art Gallery, UK

Ian Hunter
Manchester Metropolitan University, UK

Janis Jefferies
Goldsmiths, University of London, UK

Sarat Maharaj
Goldsmiths, University of London, UK

Claire Pajaczkowska
Royal College of Art, UK

John Picton
School of Oriental and African Studies, University of London, UK

Mary Schoeser
Freelance Historian, USA and UK

Caryn Simonson
Chelsea College of Art and Design, UK

Lotus Stack
Minneapolis Institute of the Arts, USA

Nick Stanley
Birmingham Institute of Art and Design, UK

Lee Talbot
The Textile Museum, USA

Sarah Taylor
University of Brighton, UK

Anne Wilson
The School of the Art Institute of Chicago, USA

Diana Wood Conroy
University of Wollongong, Australia

SUBMISSIONS

Should you have a topic you would like us to consider, please send an abstract of 300–500 words to one of the editors. Notes for Contributors can be found at the back of the journal and style guidelines are available by emailing kbruce@bergpublishers.com or from the Berg website (www.bergpublishers.com).

ISSN: 1475-9756

www.bergpublishers.com

Textile is indexed by Abstracts in Anthropology; AIO (Anthropological Index Online); ART Bibliographies Modern; British Humanities Index; Current Contents/Arts and Humanities; DAAI (Design and Applied Arts Index); IBR (International Bibliography of Book Reviews of Scholarly Literature in the Humanities and Social Sciences); IBSS (International Bibliography of the Social Sciences); IBZ (International Bibliography of Periodical Literature on the Humanities and Social Sciences); ISI Arts and Humanities Citation Index; Scopus; World Textiles.

Contents

EDITORS

Catherine Harper
School of Architecture and Design
University of Brighton
Grand Parade
Brighton BN2 4AY
UK
Catherine.Harper@brighton.ac.uk

Doran Ross
Fowler Museum at UCLA
308 Charles Young Drive
Los Angeles, CA 90095-1549
USA
dross@arts.ucla.edu

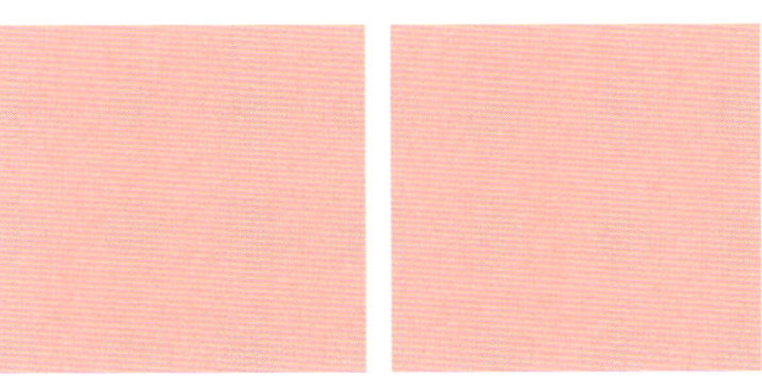

Unraveling Denim:
Introduction

Unraveling Denim: Introduction

On walking around many clothing shops, a seemingly vast array of styles of jeans are available to buy, ranging from boot cut to skinny to boyfriend, from stonewash to distressed, from pale blue to darker blue to black. At the same time there is an underlying level of homogeneity in most of the denim on sale, especially that which people wear on a daily basis. Denim itself, notwithstanding developments in textile technology, remains remarkably similar in appearance and constitution to the denim used for the first ever pairs of Levis in the nineteenth century.

It is not just that the genre is so entirely dominated by blue jeans; the basic appearance of denim is, in most cases, also conservative because of the particular way in which it is made. It is a twill fabric, woven with tightly twisted cotton yarns. Thanks to the tight twisting of the cotton yarns, the density of the fibers leads to an extremely strong, hardy and structured fabric. Denim is produced when these yarns are dyed in indigo, once natural but today synthetically produced indigo dye. As the yarns are wound so tightly, only the surface fibers are dyed, leaving the inner core of the yarns white. Only the warp yarns are dyed; the weft fibers remain white. Once the warp yarns are dyed, the fabric denim is made by interweaving warp and weft yarns together; as denim is a

SOPHIE WOODWARD
AND DANIEL MILLER

Sophie Woodward is a lecturer in sociology at the University of Manchester. She researches into material culture, consumption, clothing and personal life and has a continued interest in feminist theory and innovative methodologies. She is the author of *Why Women Wear What They Wear* (Berg, 2007) and *Why Feminism Matters* (Palgrave Macmillan, 2009 with Kath Woodward). Along with Daniel Miller, she established the Global Denim Project, and is the co-editor of *Global Denim* (Berg, 2010).

Daniel Miller is Professor of Material Culture at the Department of Anthropology, University College London. Previous work on textiles includes *Global Denim*, jointly edited with Sophie Woodward (Berg, 2010), *Clothing as Material Culture*, jointly edited with Suzanne Küchler (Berg, 2005) and *The Sari*, jointly written with Mukulika Banerjee (Berg, 2005). Other recent books include *Tales from Facebook* (Polity, 2011), *Stuff* (Polity, 2010) and *The Comfort of Things* (Polity, 2008).

Textile, Volume 9, Issue 1, pp. 6–11
DOI: 10.2752/175183511X12949158771310
Reprints available directly from the Publishers.
Photocopying permitted by licence only.

warp-faced twill fabric. This creates the conditions for its distinctive appearance. More dyed fibers are visible as the warps pass over more yarn fibers. At first this leads to a dense Indigo surface, but with attrition through wearing this can lead to an instantly recognizable pattern of fading to white in places.

In addition to the color and unique patterns of fading of denim, there are other elements that contribute to this homogenization of appearance. These include the addition of metal rivets, the original innovation of Levi-Strauss and the double lines of paler stitching. The seeming homogenization in the appearance of denim over time has lead to a lack of research into this fabric in the midst of academic research in clothing, which often focuses upon change, fashion. In this edited collection we argue that the fabric denim is worthy of more attention precisely because we also need to pay attention to such striking instances of conservatism, as represented by these continuities of denim blue jeans.

This special issue of *Textile: The Journal of Cloth and Culture* is devoted to the topic of denim. It is intended as a complement to the edited book *Global Denim* (Miller and Woodward 2010), where the main focus is upon understanding why denim jeans are so globally prevalent. Rather than take for granted that jeans are accepted as an ubiquitous presence in everyday attire in so many countries in the world, that book attempts to understand why this is so. It consists mainly of a series of ethnographic encounters. This special issue of *Textile* similarly refuses simply to take for granted

the sameness of the textile denim. As such it also aims to redress the emphasis in much of the literature on clothing that is spectacular or unusual, as if clothing that is actually worn by ordinary people is not worthy of attention or explanation.

By focusing in more depth on the textile of denim it is apparent that the fabric is beset with contradictions that are material and also symbolic. There is the initial contrast of what often starts as a hard coarse woven fabric in deep indigo blue. Yet which over time softens to white cotton threads. As the fabric itself wears down and unravels, it also changes and the contradictions appear. Denim raises contradictions between change and continuity, conformity and personalization that are core to the understanding and operation of fashion more widely.

We have therefore chosen to adopt the metaphor of "unraveling" to explore denim in this collection. When cloth and fabric are adopted as metaphors it is often to explore connectedness, in relation to ideas of the fabric of society or relationships; to talk of unraveling suggests a falling apart and the breaking of connections. In this special edition of *Textile,* all of the papers are "unraveling" denim, in the sense that they are interrogating, dissecting the many assumptions and ideas that surround the textile denim. By focusing on different aspects of the production, design, consumption and indeed the recycling of denim, these papers all, in different ways, question given associations of denim. In some instances this involves an in-depth understanding of the fibers that constitute the fabric. In other papers this implies the unraveling of practices that surround the production or wearing of jeans. As a whole the collection redresses the emphasis in much of what is written about denim and jeans already that focuses upon the images and icons of Americana. Instead, the materiality of denim is at the center of understanding.

Olesen's article helps in this regard, because it does start from the established link between jeans and America but it then notes an entirely different consequence of that link by exploring the recycling of jeans. The article engages with the so-called denim drives in America. It provides us with the most literal unraveling of the fabric denim as old jeans are processed into eco-friendly insulation. In the processing of the jeans and the acts of unraveling there is an attempt by those she investigates to create a seamless link between morality, American society and the jeans that come to embody this.

Hammer's article takes a more historical approach by looking at the Hungarian textile industry in the 1970s and at attempts to produce high-quality jeans—from early attempts to simulate the appearance of jeans through to the establishment of a Levis plant and the production of high-quality denim fabric. It offers a challenge to assumptions of either straightforward Americanization or the resistance to this. Instead the paper offers a more nuanced picture by exploring the tensions between tradition, small-scale manufacturing and technological development, and those between East and West.

Keet's paper arises from an ethnographic approach and explores the very different context of contemporary Japan, yet she similarly engages with the ways in which designers grapple with producing authentic, high-quality denim. She considers the production and consumption of "vintage" denim and unpicks the tensions between authenticity and nationality in terms of the relations between Japanese and American fabric and garments. The emphasis in this article (and for the denim "maniacs") is less on the material itself than how authenticity in denim is constructed through the way in which denim is produced.

Chakrabati's paper similarly takes an ethnographic approach to production, with the example of a jeans garment-assembly factory in Port Said in Egypt. Chakrabati develops an understanding of the materiality of the denim beyond the textile in itself, and looks at the labor processes within the factory: the tools, the action and people on the shop floor. By unraveling these practices, she highlights the complexities of shop-floor hierarchies; an illusion of unity is created in the workplace and the manufacture even if in practice it is segmented and complex.

McDonald's paper engages with similar issues of how denim may embody or allow contradictory practices and the relationship it might have to continuity and unity. However, in contrast, his paper is the only one in this collection that looks exclusively at consumption; he explores the relationship between denim consumers and kinship in contemporary China, where denim

relates to the contradictory values of tradition and transformation. Denim creates a rupture between the generations of families and the local communities but also creates connections between these same generations.

Townsend's article draws together the strands of production and consumption, by focusing upon the work of designers such as Margiela, and the author's own work, as design processes are also situated in understandings of how people wear jeans. She explores question of time, continuity yet here through the ways in which designers manipulate the surface of denim to create a sense of history and the passage of time, offering a different take on notions of "authenticity" raised in Keet's paper. What this article shows is that, once again, it is the particularity of the fabric of denim itself that matters here because it invites designers to manipulate its surface, as it is strong but can be distressed.

Compared to the edited volume *Global Denim*, this collection pays much more attention to the production of jeans and to the textile that constitutes the specifics of denim. It acknowledges the issues of symbolism and representation that are highlighted in the other collection but it adds a deeper level of enquiry into the very materiality of jeans as a textile. Olesen, for example, appears in both collections but the emphasis in her contribution here is much more towards the implications of denim as a textile, and the very fibers from which it is constructed. This materiality is clearly of utmost concern to the designers Townsend discusses and the manufacturers at the heart of Chakrabarti's paper. We did not, however, want to create an artificial dualism between academic discussions that focus only on textile and production, and those that focus on social meaning and consumption. This is why this volume directly juxtaposes these perspectives, for example, by including McDonald's study of consumption and kinship in China. Often these seem seamlessly interwoven in the accounts themselves in ways that support this academic integration. For example Hammer is concerned with historical transformations in the meaning of denim but these have much to do with the technology for the manufacture of textile. Similarly in Keet's paper the problem of precisely replicating historically important denim is actually largely a technical problem in the creation of these textiles.

So to separate out artificially the materiality of the textile and the issues of production would not be conducive to a proper understanding of either. If anything the producers of denim being studied by Keet are far more devoted to the precise symbolism and resonances of past jeans consumption than are the Chinese families who appear here as consumers. Similarly the whole premise of Olesen is that the unraveling of jeans back to fiber and its subsequent use is entirely derived from its prior symbolic quality as American. So the intention of this edited collection is that we are able to go much further in our appreciation and understanding of denim as textile and denim in production by retaining this larger integrity of the place of denim in the modern world. By the same token what this collection adds to the work on global denim is the insistence that we cannot hope to understand the history, symbolism and contemporary significance of denim without paying attention to the nature of denim as textile. Through this further integration we are starting to approach the ultimate aim of such studies, which is a better understanding of one of the most extraordinary textiles in the history of humanity – one that has shown extraordinary resilience and persistence during periods that have otherwise seen textiles come and go to a much greater extent at the behest of fashion.

Reference

Miller, Daniel and Woodward, Sophie. 2010. *Global Denim*. Oxford: Berg.

Changing the World with a Pair of Jeans: Cotton Fiber, Environmentalism and Experiential Marketing in Present-day America

Abstract

This article discusses the so-called "denim drive," an annual event in which Americans are given the opportunity to donate their old pairs of jeans, which are processed into eco-friendly insulation and used in charity projects. It discusses the emphasis on environmental concerns that is central to the drives, as well as the concerns of the main actors behind them. It also gives detailed attention to the physical, chemical and mechanical properties of cotton fiber and the transformations and applications that allow jeans to be processed into insulation. Exploring the links between the properties and transformations of cotton fibers that form the material underpinnings of the denim drives, it shows how the immense popularity of "the American uniform" facilitates the denim drives in surprising ways, which include matter as well as meaning.

Keywords: denim, recycling, cotton fiber, sustainability

BODIL BIRKEBÆK OLESEN

Bodil Birkebæk Olesen is a postdoctoral Fellow at the Department of Anthropology, Aarhus University. Her broad research interests in art and material culture and economic anthropology include publications on textile production, consumption and trade, as well as museums, and domestic interiors. She has carried out fieldwork in West Africa and the United States.

Textile, Volume 9, Issue 1, pp. 12–25
DOI: 10.2752/175183511X12949158771356
Reprints available directly from the Publishers.
Photocopying permitted by licence only.

Changing the World with a Pair of Jeans: Cotton Fiber, Environmentalism and Experiential Marketing in Present-day America

This article discusses the so-called "denim drive," an annual event in which Americans are given the opportunity to donate their old pairs of jeans, which are processed into eco-friendly insulation and used in charity projects. These drives provide an interesting perspective on a relatively overlooked aspect of "the American uniform" (Sullivan 2006: 8): while much of the existing literature on the significance of jeans in America addresses the semiotics of wearing the garment (for example Botterill 2007; Comstock 2010; Davis 1989), the practices of disposal and recycling that are central to the drives provide an opportunity to explore a particular aspect of jeans' materiality, namely their existence as cotton fiber. Discussing aspects of fiber qualities and textile engineering, I explore the links between the properties and transformations of cotton fibers that form the material underpinnings of the denim drives. As I will show, the immense popularity of the American uniform facilitates the denim drives in surprising ways, which include matter as well as meaning.

From Blue to Green—The Denim Drives

In September 2005, Cotton Incorporated, a research and marketing company funded by American cotton producers and importers, launched its Cotton's Dirty Laundry Tour.[1] Part of a US$27 million advertising and promotional push it intended to sow loyalty among young consumers by creating awareness of cotton as a versatile, easy-care product that is ideally suited for the demands of American college students. Organized as one-day campus events at ten colleges across the country, and spiced up with music, fashion shows and games, the tour provided basic activities and information about cotton garments and their care to American youngsters who, as the organizers explained in a press release, "may be doing their own laundry for the first time in their lives."[2] When the tour was repeated in 2006, this time visiting fourteen college campuses, it included a supplementary promotional campaign named Cotton From Blue to Green, or simply the "denim drive."[3] Whereas the Cotton's

Dirty Laundry Tour was meant to communicate to college students that jeans, as the promotional material put it, were "cool and comfortable,"[4] the Cotton From Blue to Green campaign highlighted another aspect of cotton's many qualities, namely that it was "natural, renewable and recyclable."[5] Through this campaign Cotton Inc., according to a press release, showed its commitment to the environment by "producing and participating in … special projects that communicate the importance of minimizing harm on the environmental footprint by being natural, sustainable, responsible and renewable."[6] The concept of the campaign was simple: students were asked to donate their old jeans, which, once collected, would be turned into Ultra Touch, a so-called eco-friendly building insulation material used by the Baton Rouge branch of Habitat for Humanity in the construction of houses for families whose homes were destroyed by Hurricane Katrina in 2005. As an additional incentive to participate in the denim drive, the Buckle, an apparel retailer operating more than 300 stores across the US, offered coupons worth $5 off the purchase of a pair of jeans for every piece of denim donated to the campaign.[7] The opportunity to donate their jeans created by the denim drive, a representative explained, "shows students the benefits of a natural, renewable fabric as well as how easy it is to do something for the environment and contribute their own bit."[8]

In 2007 a retail extension was added to the college campus activities of the campaign. The

retailer partnership included Gap, which donated unused denim fabric, as well Guess by Marciano, who gave a 10 percent discount towards the purchase of new jeans to all customers donating a piece of old denim at any of the store locations.[9] Guess by Marciano's campaign to help meet its goal of 5,000 donated pieces of denim, according to a spokesperson for Guess, "symbolizes our commitment to the people and groups we interact with … it illustrates the Guess by Marciano brand's true DNA as being more than just about fashion."[10] In 2008 Cotton's Dirty Laundry Tour was discontinued but the denim drive expanded further, including more retailers as well as inviting businesses and companies to donate collected denim to the drive.[11] The two prominent jeans retailers, National Jean Company and Earnest Sewn, launched their Make an Earnest Difference five-day charity denim drive in National Jean Company's New York stores. The drive was launched with a fashion show in New York in April and culminated with in-store events at National Jean Company's Long Island and Manhattan locations, featuring fashion experts and celebrities who offered fashion advice and participated in various fashion games. In return for their donations, customers received a 20 percent discount that could be used to purchase a new pair of jeans at any National Jean Company store. That year 38,275 pieces of denim were collected, more than twice the amount (14,566) collected in 2006 and slightly more than the 36,958 pieces collected in 2007.[12] In 2009, the drive also received

more than 33,088 pieces of denim from *National Geographic Kids Magazine,* which had asked its readers to donate their used denim, a request that was given further impetus as a Guinness World Record for the Largest Collection of Clothes to Recycle.[13] By the end of 2009 the website announced that more than 180,000 pieces of denim had been collected, and the nearly 90,000 pieces of denim collected by 2008 had been used to insulate 180 homes in the Gulf Coast region.[14] The denim drive was to continue in 2010, once again giving Americans the opportunity to become involved and thus, as the campaign slogan put it, "Change the world one pair of jeans at a time."[15]

The straightforwardness of the philanthropic act evoked by the slogan—that individuals can help the environment and people in need by giving away a pair of jeans—is articulated visually on the campaign website. Predominantly in white, blue and green, the background features and main images conjure up a tripartite connectivity—of cotton bolls, of jeans and of eco-friendly building insulation—whose symbiotic relationship is further suggested by the presence of the three chasing arrows of the recycling symbol to their left. The center image—an anonymous female holding a globe, clear blue oceans and lush green continents partly hidden beneath soft white clouds, in front of her—lends further credence to the suggestion that the acts and objects in question, and the relationship between them, are the very elements that make up a healthy planet. Placed above these images, the campaign logo accompanying the slogan repeats these suggestions in a compressed form: the seal of cotton, Cotton Incorporated's trademark (see below), in white, is encircled from below by the campaign slogan, and from above by an arrow whose color changes gradually from blue to green, once again conveying a seamless fit between cotton, jeans, and environmental wellbeing, which allows the world to be changed for the better pair by pair of jeans.

The drives themselves dramatize this cycle and the successive relationship between cotton, jeans, and eco-friendly insulation, emphasizing recycling as an act— that of giving away a pair of jeans or other denim garments. In fact, it seems to be this very act that keeps the cycle going and thus makes the world a better, greener place. This positive message is perhaps not surprising, given that the denim drive is a promotional campaign launched by an organization whose successful creation of a market for the product it is meant to secure is partly the result of continuously aligning the product with important collective values—and given that the campaign was partly developed in collaboration with a leading agency in branding and experiential marketing. Before addressing this collaboration in more detail, however, I want to address recycling not as an act of disposal or donation as presented in the drives but as the reprocessing of material to prevent waste, reduce the use of resources and reduce pollution. I shall explore various aspects of why and how denim is turned into insulation material. Throwing light on this involves addressing what cotton is and what it does and how it is made to do it—questions that usually fall within the confines of textile engineering rather than the social sciences or the humanities.

From the Sociology of Clothing to the Engineering of Fibrous Materials

As mentioned above, understanding the material transformations of recycling involves addressing cotton from a textile engineering perspective, in which cotton first and foremost is a fibrous material with a wide variety of characteristics that determine what can and cannot be done with it. The main constituent of cotton and other vegetable fibers is cellulose, a polymer or macromolecule that is also the major constituent of paper and cardboard. It is the particular arrangement of polymers into long chains that determines a fiber's chemical, physical and mechanical properties such as strength, elongation, and absorbance (Broughton and Brady 1995a: 31; Collier and Tortora 2000: 234). Like other vegetable fibers such as flax, and protein fibers such as wool and silk, cotton fiber is suitable for textile applications because it has sufficient length, strength, and flexibility to be turned into yarn—that is, twisted or otherwise held together with other fibers in a continuous strand (Collier and Tortora 2000: 47, 242). And like rayon, a manufactured cellulose fiber, cotton has excellent absorbing qualities and is commonly used in the fabrication of disposable care items such as baby diapers, cotton tips, tampons, paper towels and facial wipes.

The disposal of a garment may mark the end of its utility for its owner but from a textile engineering perspective it remains a fibrous material with a range of properties, giving it potential for further applications. Such applications may be limited by the fact that the fiber has been used for clothing and its utility may be limited to cases where the novelty of the fiber is not crucial or the aesthetic properties of the fabric are less important than utility and cost (Santvoort 1994: 81). For example, garments that are unsuited for second-hand use due to wear and tear may be cut into smaller patches and sold as industrial wipers, an application for which absorbing qualities are paramount.

In other cases, such as with pre-consumer waste, which often consists of fabric clippings whose shape and size make them unsuited as wipes, one way of unleashing their economic and material potential is by processing them into their original fibrous state. Fabrics undergoing this processing are subjected to the action of disintegrating machines, which pull the rags apart and break them by tearing and shredding them, and then to a succession of garnet machines of increasing fineness whereby the threads that composed the original textile are unraveled into their constituent fibers (see Matos 1914). This process, however, compromises the mechanical properties of the fiber making it unsuited for yarn production unless it is mixed with other fibers. India is home to the production of low-quality acrylic blankets using such reclaimed fibers (Norris 2005) and in the US such fibers are generally used for other applications that exploit a variety of the fibers' material properties. Such applications include stuffing for mattresses and pillows, use as carpet underlay or floor padding and the manufacture of geotextiles (Adanur 1995). For many of these applications the reclaimed fiber is processed into so-called non-wovens, sheets, webs or bats of fibers that are bonded to each other by methods other than knitting or weaving (Broughton and Brady 1995b: 141). These means of bonding include stitching, adding an adhesive such as resin to the fiber material, or fusing it thermally or chemically (Santvoort 1994: 68). In order to tailor the qualities of such non-wovens to their particular application, different fibers can be mixed, and the material can be given chemical treatments. They can be produced as roll goods or, as is often the case in the automotive industry, they can be produced in large moulds designed for their particular application, for example, as insulation in a car door.

In addition to the properties of particular fibers and the technological possibilities for tailoring them to particular ends, the possible applications of a fibrous material also depend on a range of socio-economic factors such as aesthetic preferences, supply and demand, and national and international legislation. In other words, the selection of fibers to a considerable degree determines the properties of the final non-woven product but they are selected according to customer requirements, costs and other factors. Wool, for example— because of its natural fire-resistant qualities—has received new interest and higher prices as stuffing as European flammability legislation for upholstered furnishings and protective clothing has demanded higher wool content (Hawley 2006: 268). By the same token, reclaimed fiber was commonly used to manufacture carpet underlay and door panels in the automotive industry until rising oil prices prompted manufacturers to reduce the weight of their vehicles.[16] Synthetic materials thus became a favored option and, as the non-woven industry in the US has made a number of technological advances, it has been able to deliver highly specified non-wovens in a speedy, cost-efficient and tailor-made manner. More recently the cost of landfill and other environmental concerns has sparked in interest in finding biodegradable and recycled solutions in the automotive industry, heightening the interest in waste cotton fiber. One important reason behind the installment of carpet underlay, floor-coverings, package trays, door panels, head and trunk liners are their sound-absorbing properties, that is their capacity to reduce noise inside the passenger compartment. Recent research has explored the use of natural fiber non-wovens for floor coverings, among them waste cotton, whose acoustical absorption performance is at par with existing products but is bio-degradable and therefore more environmentally benign (Parikh *et al.* 2006).

The properties of reclaimed fiber material and the socio-economic factors that influence its potential applications are similarly implicated in the utility and commercial viability of Ultra Touch, the insulation material produced from the jeans collected in the denim drives. The insulation material is manufactured and patented by Bonded Logic in Chandler, Arizona, a company that manufactures and markets thermal and acoustical insulation products for application in a wide range of industries including the automotive, appliance and building industries. A main purpose of such applications is to control temperature and often also sound in homes, commercial buildings and industrial operations as well as for air ducts, pipers, walls, floors, automobiles, fridges and domestic cooking appliances. Such insulation reduces the energy needed to heat and cool buildings. It reduces the rate of heat transfer between the inside and outside of a building essentially by preventing heat from entering or escaping from a building. Heat is primarily transferred through conduction as neighboring molecules within or between substances are in direct contact with each other, thus allowing energy to flow between them (Incropera and DeWitt 2002: 3–4). A building insulation material such as fiberglass is a good insulator because of the tiny pockets of air trapped between its fibers, keeping the air still and thus transferring less energy. The ability of insulation to slow the transfer of heat is often measured and expressed in so-called R-values: the higher the R-value of an insulation material the better its ability to resist the flow of heat through it.[17]

Cotton fiber can be engineered to perform in a similar way to conventional insulation materials, and Ultra Touch, the insulation material featured in the denim drives, is made with 85 percent reclaimed cotton, mainly from denim waste from the Mexican blue jeans industry. The waste is first transported to the US where it processed by a garnetter in order to return it to its fibrous state prior to its manufacture at Bonded Logic. Once reclaimed the fiber is treated with a fireproofing solution, mixed with polyolefin fibers, which melt and bond the material together as a non-woven bat when the mixture is heated, and then extruded for the engineered density and thickness according to the different recommended R-values for insulation material for walls, ceilings and floors.[18] Ultra Touch has the same thermal qualities as conventional insulation material, as well as better acoustical qualities. And while it is 30 percent to 50 percent more expensive than such conventional materials, it is free of the formaldehyde and other toxic elements of conventional insulation products that are believed to potentially cause asthma and allergies.[19] In the context of growing environmental concerns, the use of reclaimed cotton fiber, derived from post-industrial waste that otherwise could have been consigned to landfills, for the manufacture of Ultra Touch, is an important reason for its commercial viability despite its higher price. The numerous websites providing a variety of information relating to sustainable building construction, such as greenbuildingadvisor. com, greenhomeguide.com or buildinggreen.com, as well as the many retailers specializing in sustainable building materials, are one indication of consumer interest in building or maintaining their homes with materials that put fewer strains on the environment. The US Green Building Council, a non-profit trade organization that promotes sustainability in the design, construction, and operation of buildings, created the first national green building certification system known as LEED—Leadership in Energy and Environmental Design—in 1998, and since then various initiatives ranging from legislation to tax incentives have been introduced by federal agencies, state governments, and city councils throughout the country.[20] For example, the Rhode Island Green Building Act requires all new public agency building projects, as well as major projects of public schools districts across the state receiving state funding, to achieve LEED certification.[21]

"Doing Your Bit"—Experiential Marketing and Post-industrial Waste

Although brief, this exploration of the material properties of cotton fiber, and the way in which they can be put to use in various applications, does give a sense of some of the material connections and transformations of cotton fiber, denim textile, and their recycling that, although implicated, remain somewhat invisible in the denim drives. Moreover, the very specific, material requirements that underwrite the manufacture and marketing of Ultra Touch as a sustainable insulation product also provide a useful point of comparison for the environmentalism articulated and practiced in the denim drives. As described above, while it is the fibrous nature of cotton that is exploited in its application as insulation, it is the ability of reclaimed cotton waste to perform at par with conventional insulation materials that, in a context of a green certification system, for example, allows it to promote itself as green or eco-friendly. Or, to put it differently, it is because its manufacture, based on a reclaimed fiber product, puts less strain on environmental resources and reduces landfill, compared to conventional insulation products, that it is characterized as green. In the denim drives, while the eco-friendliness of Ultra Touch is occasionally mentioned, it is the eco-friendliness of cotton itself that is the crucial point. As described above, the opportunity to donate jeans or denim in the drives is presented as an opportunity to become familiar with the benefits of a natural, renewable fabric as well as an opportunity to do something for the environment. Thus, the argument seems to go, within the setup of the denim drive, the act of donation exposes the consumers to information about the eco-friendliness of jeans or denim and, by extension, of cotton in general, the most remarkable one being its applicability for reclaimed cotton insulation. In addition to this the donation itself is the act that allows the consumer to improve the current state of the environment because his or her donation is used to manufacture eco-friendly insulation material.

Leaving the premises of this argument about the inherent eco-friendliness of cotton and jeans donation aside for now, its seemingly straightforward and unambiguous message is hardly surprising given that the drives are the promotional events of the company whose *raison d'être* is to improve the demand for and profitability of cotton. Cotton Incorporated was established in 1970 at a point in time where cotton had undergone a steady decline in apparel market shares to synthetic fibers from 65 percent in 1960 to 33 percent in 1970. A crucial element in the company's successful efforts at recapturing cotton's market share has been its creation of a trademark, the now well-known Seal of Cotton, which had garnered more than 700 licenses by 2001 (Jacobson and Smith 2001: 165). The ubiquity of the seal has been used to create a branded identification not of a manufacturer or of Cotton Incorporated but of the material, cotton itself, an identification that for many years built on the distinct performance characteristics of cotton fibers to highlight their sensuous qualities. "Wearing it [makes] you feel good" (Jacobson and Smith 2001: 183) is a selling point that was emphasized creatively and repeatedly in the company's advertising and promotional efforts since the establishment of the trademark. Within this branding strategy of emphasizing the unique qualities of cotton fiber, these were deliberately pitted against synthetic ones, and the connotations of natural fibers (from plant, animal or mineral sources as opposed to synthetic fibers) were linked to cotton's performance characteristics such as softness, durability, smell as well as the performance of cotton garments when subject to tumble drying or ironing. These brand identification efforts continue today and according to the company itself more than 80 percent of all Americans recognize the Seal of Cotton.[22] More recently, however, recognizing the growing environmental concerns among its customers, a large proportion of the more than $20 million spent on advertising and promotional activities every year has been used to realign the brand with eco-friendliness and environmental sustainability.[23] In this context much effort has gone into expanding customer associations of the natural qualities of cotton. Thus, previous efforts directed at articulating the natural qualities of cotton in opposition to synthetic materials and aligning them with notions of comfort and quality, are now combined with efforts to brand cotton as recyclable and renewable.

This dual pursuit is easily detected in the coupling of "cool and comfortable" with "natural, renewable and recyclable" that was used to describe the tandem existence of Cottons Dirty Laundry Tour and the denim drive. Both campaigns were developed in collaboration with Jack Morton, an agency specializing in experiential marketing. Experiential marketing creates brand identification through the staging of events or activities that facilitate a more interactive consumer engagement with a brand than what is allowed for in more conventional advertising. And Jack Morton has designed a large number of innovative, award-winning experiential ad campaigns for a wide variety of companies and institutions ranging from Nokia

and Statoil to the September 11 Foundation. When the American Commerce department launched an estimated $340 million campaign to promote the 2010 US Census, Jack Morton organized its first phase, the so-called US Census 2010 *Portrait of America* Road Tour, for which thirteen vehicles would travel across the nation, engage audiences in a variety of events to share images and stories and explain how the census works and the positive impact people's participation can have on their local community and the nation.[24] As explained above, both Cottons Dirty Laundry Tour and the denim drive were organized around a similarly positive message and brought to the audience through their immediate and direct engagement in various activities. The original target group, American college students, was described as the "millennium generation," estimated to spend $140 millions annually,[25] and nurturing their lifelong loyalty to cotton products has been identified as crucial in sustaining and expanding the market for cotton (Jacobson and Smith 2001: 172). Incorporating jeans, the American uniform by definition for this segment of the population, as part of the interactive experience in these campaigns facilitated the success of the campaigns in a number of ways. As I have argued elsewhere, the amplified resonance of the garment in American culture and its complicity in sustaining normative collective values makes its alignment with environmental concerns very powerful (Olesen 2010). Jeans already occupied a special position in Cotton Incorporated's marketing efforts as the American consumers first and foremost valued encounter with cotton garments, a status that could be built on when nurturing American teenagers' continued loyalty to and preference for cotton garments (Jacobson and Smith 2001: 174). The donation of jeans in the campaigns thus worked to emphasize the goodness of green and, by extension, of cotton and it made the campaigns stand out in the minds of consumers. Moreover, as in-house research had shown that the average American owns nine pair of jeans, the likelihood that everyone would have a pair that he or she was willing to give away—and a willingness to replace them with a new pair—was high. In other words, the denim drive is a remarkable marketing achievement as it both demonstrates and brands the "benefits" of a recyclable material like cotton, and simultaneously engages the consumers in this positive benefit by allowing them to donate their own jeans to an environmentally (and socially) good cause while incorporating the continued consumption of cotton garments as an integral part of exercising environmental awareness. Or at least the marketing success of the drives seems to be indicated by the discontinuation of the Cottons Dirty Laundry Tour and the continuation and expansion of the drives to include more and more consumer segments year by year.

Whether the drives can be said to be a similarly outstanding achievement from the perspective of reducing waste or the use of resources in the production of new consumer goods is perhaps more open to debate. A core argument

among the critics of corporations' engagement with environmental issues has been the way in which these always posit continued, if not increasing, consumption as entirely compatible with environmental sustainability (see, for example, Smith 1996, 1998; Todd 2004). In line with this thinking, it could be argued that the incentive to replace every donated piece of denim with a new one presents a distorted view of environmental sustainability that, moreover, glosses over how and why recycling may contribute to such sustainability as well as what is entailed in the notion that a resource is renewable. Given that the average American disposes of 68 pounds of clothing and textiles every year the environment might be better off if consumers restricted themselves to wearing one of their remaining eight pairs.[26] Moreover, the denim used in the manufacture of Ultra Touch is normally post-industrial waste derived from manufacturing units rather than the post-consumer denim waste that accumulates when consumers dispose of unwanted used denim garments. Reclaiming fiber from post-consumer rather than post-industrial waste is more difficult as, for example, zippers and buttons must be removed prior to the processing of the fabric and its sourcing is more expensive for the manufacturer.[27] In fact, 25 percent all post-consumer waste processed by the US textile recycling industry is turned into wipers as described above while only 7 percent is reprocessed.[28] From this perspective, the educational point that jeans can be recycled as insulation may be a great way of catching attention but it does

little in terms of conveying how recycling works in practice and what happens to jeans that are not donated to the drive. Against this it could be argued that such a critique is equally flawed in its view of what counts as environmentally benign and that the great potential of these campaigns is to create awareness among young American consumers, motivating them to make more informed choices in their consumption patterns throughout their lives, and that such awareness is built only through a clear, concise message that cannot address the complexity of environmental sustainability. If nothing else it could be argued that the jeans donated at least are not consigned to landfill.

The 180,000 pieces of denim collected in the denim drives by the end of 2009 may at first seem like a staggering number but is perhaps less impressive if one takes into account that Bonded Logic uses more than 300 tons of denim waste, roughly equivalent to 400,000 pairs of jeans, a month for the manufacture of Ultra Touch. This suggests that the number of jeans or denim collected in the drives constitutes a minuscule proportion of the denim garments currently produced or owned. These numbers could easily provide grounds for discussing the advantages and disadvantages of the campaigns, but the figures also point to another dimension of cotton fiber and its properties from an engineering perspective, namely their sourcing and availability. Central to the performance of insulation material is the way in which it reduces heat transfer essentially by trapping air within its fiber and keeping it still.

Length and fineness are crucial for a fibrous material's ability to do this as it is within the interconnected loops and curls between fibers that air is trapped. When sourcing a reclaimed fiber—as opposed to manufacturing a fibrous material to particular specifications—this favors the use of reclaimed fibers from fabrics with a relatively small number of rather tightly twisted fibers in their yarns, partly because extracting fibers of such coarser and less twisted yarn is less costly than yarns with more and finer fibers in their cross-section.[29] Both reclaimed wool and cotton fibers from a wide range of fabrics fulfill these requirements but have a number of disadvantages. Wool, firstly, makes up a mere 3 percent of the world production of fibers compared to the 40 percent of cotton, generally making wool fiber more expensive and limiting its availability.[30] Secondly, from the perspective of cost and availability, denim fabric has a number of advantages compared to other cotton materials. Ironically, the immense popularity of denim, and particularly jeans, also makes denim waste a readily available and relatively inexpensive waste material. The number of denim garments produced and the manner in which they are produced is implicated in this because cutting the fabric for jeans generates large quantities of textile waste. As a roll-good, denim is cut into a number of identical pieces, stacked, and cut in the exact shape needed, producing a lot of trim waste and thus a readily available fabric material for reprocessing. In addition to this, the presence of a large number of jeans manufacturers in Mesoamerica minimizes transportation costs. Some of these manufacture more than 20,000 pairs of jeans a day. In 2000, jeans manufacturing firms in the region surrounding the city of Torreon in northern Mexico alone produced an average of more than four million pairs of jeans a week (Bair and Gereffi 2001).

Conclusion

In this article I have explored some of the material, commercial, environmental and cultural underpinnings of the denim drives and their call to "change the world one pair of jeans at a time." Central to this exploration has been attention to the cotton fiber, the substance matter of both jeans and recycled cotton insulation. Capable of being twisted into yarn, woven into denim and sewn into jeans, it is this fibrous material's ability to subsequently be shredded, unraveled, and re-bonded to trap air according to specified measures on which the drives rely. The semiotic density of jeans in the US and their concomitant suitability for evoking an intimate experience of moral American being makes them the ideal signifier of environmental concern for those who are trying to "brand" cotton as green (Olesen 2010). Moreover, as a common feature in the American wardrobe, they are available to be given away by individual Americans in the drives, creating that crucial experiential moment of metamorphosis where the greenness of the recycled insulation material becomes a quality of the consumer through his or her act of donation. But the immense popularity of the

American uniform facilitates the drives in other ways: the properties of the fiber and the symbolic connotations of the garment converge in surprising ways, as it is its popularity that fosters the abundance of uniform post-industrial cotton fiber waste on which the manufacture of cotton insulation relies. While attention to the physical, chemical and mechanical properties of cotton fiber, its transformations and applications, may at first seem at odds with a sociological concern with the significance of a garment, its meaning and its agency, it allows us to grasp the political economic context in which such meaning and agency unfolds and the materials and material transformations that make green more than a color.

Notes

1. See http://promomagazine. com/news/cotton_ tour_091505/index.html (accessed April 21, 2009).
2. See www.accesscotton.com/ (accessed March 23, 2008).
3. See www.cottoninc.com/ PressReleases/?articleID=392 (accessed March 2008).
4. See www. cottonfrombluetogreen.org/ Cotton-From-Blue-To-Green-Program-History/ (accessed March 2008).
5. See www. cottonfrombluetogreen.org/ Cotton-From-Blue-To-Green-Program-History/ (accessed March 2008).
6. See www.cottoninc.com/ PressReleases/?articleID=460 (accessed April 21, 2009).
7. See www.cottoninc.com/ PressReleases/?articleID=392 (accessed March 2008).
8. See www.cottoninc.com/ PressReleases/?articleID=461 (accessed April 21, 2009).
9. See www.cottoninc.com/ PressReleases/?articleID=445 (accessed December 20, 2010).
10. See www.cottoninc.com/ PressReleases/?articleID=440 (accessed December 20, 2010).
11. See www. cottonfrombluetogreen.org/ Cotton-From-Blue-To-Green-Program-History/ (accessed February 4, 2010).
12. See www. cottonfrombluetogreen.org/ Houses-Built/ (accessed February 4, 2010).
13. See www.cottoninc.com/ pressreleases/?articleID=499 (accessed December 20, 2010). http://kids. nationalgeographic.com/ Stories/MoreStories/ Guinness-clothes and www. thefabricofourlives.com/ for-the-children/New-Guiness-World-Record/ (accessed February 4, 2010).
14. See www. cottonfrombluetogreen.org/ (accessed February 4, 2010).
15. See www. cottonfrombluetogreen.org/ (accessed February 4, 2010).
16. Interview with American garnetter, April 23, 2008.
17. R-value is measured in Kelvin square meters per watt.
18. See www.bondedlogic. com/ultratouch-cotton.htm (accessed April 15, 2008).
19. See, for example, www. greenlivingtips.com/ articles/62/1/Toxic-formaldehyde.html (accessed December 20, 2010).
20. See www.usgbc. org/DisplayPage. aspx?CMSPageID=1852 (accessed February 4, 2010).
21. See www.rilin.state.ri.us// BillText09/SenateText09/ S0232B.pdf Rhode Island Green Building Act (accessed January 15, 2010).
22. See www.cottoninc.com/ PressReleases/?articleID=39 (accessed February 4, 2010).
23. See www.cottoninc.com/ PressReleases/?articleID=41 (accessed April 21, 2009).
24. See http://mediadecoder. blogs.nytimes. com/2010/01/04/advertising-census-working-overtime/ and http://2010.census. gov/2010census/roadtour/ (accessed February 4, 2010).
25. See www.cottoninc.com/ PressReleases/?articleID=349 (accessed April 21, 2009).
26. The figure of 68 pounds is provided by the Secondary Materials and Recycled Textiles Association, see www. textilerecycle.org/ (accessed December 20, 2010).
27. The lack of precise information on the exact (synthetic) contents of a piece of castoff clothing also limits its possible applications to those where the exact fiber content is irrelevant, just as the need to control very specific properties in order to engineer the necessary properties of the insulation material favors the use of post-industrial reclaimed fiber material.
28. Thirty-five percent of the post-consumer textile waste

that is recycled is exported as second-hand clothing, while 26 percent is exported as textile waste to be reprocessed. Only 7 percent is consigned to landfill. These figures are provided by the Secondary Materials and Recycled Textiles Association, see www.textilerecycle.org/.

29. Interview with American garnetter, 23 April 2008.

30. World Fiber—Trends in Demand and Supply 2007. Industry report published by Yarns and Fibre, pp. 8, 14.

References

Adanur, Sabit. 1995. "Geotextiles." In S. Adanur (ed.) *Wellington Sears Handbook of Industrial Textiles*. Lancaster, PA: Technomic Publishing Company.

Bair, Jennifer and Gereffi, Gary. 2001. "Local Clusters in Global Chains: The Causes and Consequences of Export Dynamism in Torreon's Blue Jeans Industry." *World Development* 29(11): 1885–903.

Botterill, Jacqueline. 2007. "Cowboys, Outlaws and Artists: The Rhetoric of Authenticity and Contemporary Jeans and Sneaker Advertisements." *Journal of Consumer Culture* 7(1): 105–25.

Broughton, R. M., and Brady, P. H. 1995a. "Fiber Forming Polymers." In S. Adanur (ed.) *Wellington Sears Handbook of Industrial Textiles*. Lancaster, PA: Technomic Publishing Company.

Broughton, R. M., and Brady, P. H. 1995b. "Nonwoven Fabrics." In S. Adanur (ed.) *Wellington Sears Handbook of Industrial Textiles*, Lancaster, PA: Technomic Publishing Company.

Collier, Billie J. and Phyllis Tortora, G. 2000. *Understanding Textiles*. Upper Saddle River, NJ: Prentice-Hall.

Comstock, Sandra. 2010. "The Making of an American Icon: The Transformation of Blue Jeans during the Great Depression." In Daniel Miller and Sophie Woodward (eds) *Global Denim*. Oxford: Berg.

Davis, Fred. 1989. "Of Maids' Uniforms and Blue Jeans: The Drama of Status Ambivalences in Clothing and Fashion." *Qualitative Sociology* 12(4): 337–55.

Hawley, Jana M. 2006. "Digging for Diamonds: A Conceptual Framework for Understanding Reclaimed Textile Products." *Clothing and Textiles* 24(3): 262–75.

Incropera, Frank P. and David P. DeWitt. 2002. *Fundamentals of Heat and Mass Transfer*. New York: John Wiley & Sons, Inc.

Jacobson, Timothy Curtis, and George David Smith. 2001. *Cotton's Renaissance: A Study in Market Innovation*. Cambridge: Cambridge University Press.

Matos, Louis Joseph. 1914. "Shoddy and Carbonized Waste." *Journal of Industrial and Engineering Chemistry* 6(9): 765–7.

Norris, Lucy. 2005. "Cloth that Lies: The Secrets of Recycling in India." In S. Küchler and D. Miller (eds) *Clothing as Material Culture*. Oxford: Berg.

Olesen, Bodil Birkebæk. 2010. "How Blue Jeans Went Green: The Materiality of an American Icon." In Daniel Miller and Sophie Woodward (eds) *Global Denim*. Oxford: Berg.

Parikh, D. V., Chen, Y. and Sun, L. 2006. "Reducing Automotive Interior Noise with Natural Fiber Nonwoven Floor Covering Systems." *Textile Research Journal* 76(11): 813–20.

Santvoort, Gerard P. T. M. van. (ed.) 1994. *Geotextiles and Geomembrances in Civil Engineering*. Rotterdam: Balkema.

Smith, Neil. 1996. "The Production of Nature." In G. Robertson, J. Bird, B. Curtis and M. Mash (eds) *FutureNatural: Nature, Science, Culture*. London: Routledge.

Smith, Toby. 1998. *The Myth of Green Marketing: Tending our Goats at the Edge of the Apocalypse*. Toronto: University of Toronto Press.

Sullivan, James. 2006. *Jeans: A Cultural History of an American Icon*. New York: Gotham Books.

Todd, Anne Marie. 2004. "The Aesthetic Turn in Green Marketing: Environmental Consumer Ethics of Natural Personal Care Products." *Ethics and the Environment* 9(2): 86–102.

Magyar Denim: Metamorphoses in the Clothing Factory

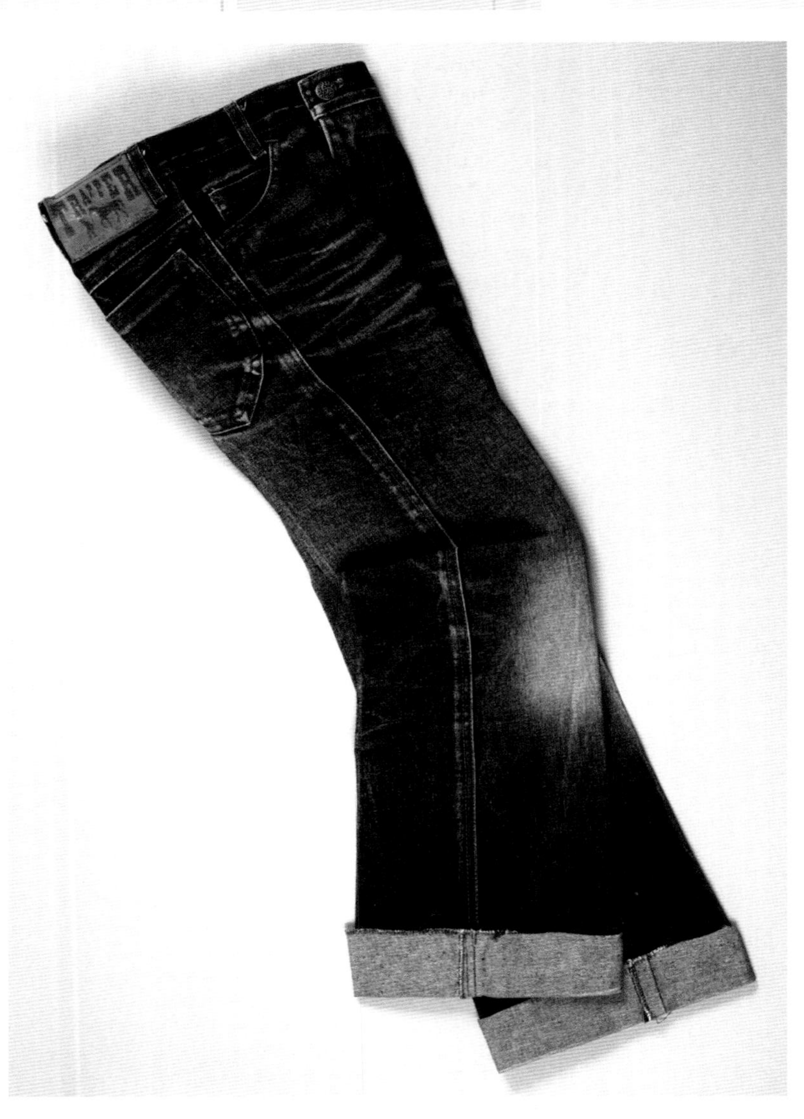

Abstract

In this article, based on contemporary press coverage analysis and my interviews with retired industry workers and leaders, I outline the initial phase of the production of denim jeans in Hungary in the late 1970s. This process involved a range of attempts to set conditions for mass manufacturing of denim jeans, which often collided with everyday realities in the non-market-driven economic circumstances prevailing in the Eastern Bloc. Whether it was the production of a heavy cotton twill of standard quality, or the dyeing that makes the worn jeans look as they should, or a marketing practice that could make Eastern-made jeans appealing to consumers—these goals often turned out to be difficult for Hungarian manufacturers. In my analysis of three companies' attempts to produce jeans I outline some problems in establishing a production practice with technological and management standards set by Western-branded jeans—all well known by Hungarian customers—in the regulatory and technological environment of a socialist planned economy. These attempts to produce jeans—some of which were, in fact, quite successful—in retrospect served a variety of objectives for those involved, whether they were the technocratic reform agendas of socialist industry chiefs or a meaningful life for shop-floor workers.

Keywords: Cold War, denim, textile manufacturing, communism, economic modernization, Levi Strauss & Co.

FERENC HAMMER

Ferenc Hammer has a PhD in sociology and is an assistant professor at ELTE University's Institute for Art Theory and Media Studies in Budapest. His recent research interest concerns the acts and processes of conceptualizing objects and material in general in everyday life.

Textile, Volume 9, Issue 1, pp. 26–43
DOI: 10.2752/175183511X12949158771392
Reprints available directly from the Publishers.
Photocopying permitted by licence only.
© 2011 Berg. Printed in the United Kingdom.

Magyar Denim: Metamorphoses in the Clothing Factory

Introduction

In this study I describe and analyze the process of the increasing capitalization of the ever-growing popular interest in denim by the Hungarian textile industry from the early 1970s. I outline the hesitant early fashion design profession and industry attempts—following a period of neglect in which denim wearing in public could lead to prosecution—to legitimize denim as a durable work and leisure outfit, and industry experiments by now largely defunct textile and clothing works to manufacture raw materials to fulfill the increasingly sophisticated demand for quality denim. The key part of this article is the description and interpretation of the making and functioning of the Levi's plant in Hungary in 1978. I present a colorful array of often amusingly conflicting goals and motivations by looking at the strategies of Hungarian officials and textile industry leaders, the workers themselves, the media, and officials at Levi Strauss & Co. In the course of the analysis I place particular emphasis on the treatment of the production of Levi's in personal recollections, archival materials and media pieces, as their vision of politics offers an alternative to the usual Cold War narratives of jeans production behind the Iron Curtain. Archival sources regarding the operation of the denim manufacturers that I analyze in this study are scarce because most of them have been liquidated by now and very often—despite archival regulations in Hungary— the documentation has been lost. Key elements of my sources are the six interviews I made with retired textile professionals who, as top managers, textile engineers or shopfloor forewomen, played significant roles making the denim industry in the late 1970s.

The Shift

Valóság (Reality), the respected social science journal of the 1844-founded Society for the Dissemination of Scientific Knowledge, published a one-page open letter by playwright and theater director László Gyurkó (1971) addressed to the Central Committee of KISZ (Communist Youth Organization) in its July 1971 issue. Gyurkó, a freshly elected MP, weighty cultural policy broker and subsequently influential biographer/propagandist of Party leader János Kádár,[1] had chosen a somewhat unusual subject for the pages of the social science review: the dress and entry code of a popular Budapest youth entertainment venue (Buda Youth Park), with particular attention to men's long hair and jeans. Gyurkó contended in his letter that the Party and the Communist Youth Organization should refrain from policing young people's clothing unless they wish to take the risk that "consequently the youth may even question the truly important and necessary constraints of their life." Gyurkó's cultural policy cameo not only highlights the deep structures of politics and agency in the *détente* period, or "soft dictatorship" in the Cold War but also marks a significant change in the official attitude concerning the wearing of blue jeans. The 1960s had witnessed a slow liberalization of youth clothing worn in public spaces, particularly jeans. While in the first part of the 1960s hooliganism—that is, politically motivated deviance—had been often associated with American denim in the press, in the latter years of the 1960s jeans had become gradually accepted in pictures appearing in youth magazines or on record covers (Hammer 2008). In a sense, as suggested by Gyurkó's comment quoted above, actors in the cultural policy sphere, without any particular coordination, had weighed the costs and benefits of the regulation of jeans in public life, in the press and in policing appearance in public venues, and realized that outfit liberalization may offer far more benefits than the perceived orderliness of jean-less public spaces.[2] As discussed in Hammer (2008), an important starting point of the relaxing process in appearance regulation was the Seventh Congress of the KISZ in July 1967 when Party First Secretary János Kádár himself warned hardline conservatives that "Wild-West pants, beards, or hairstyles" are not the most important cultural policy issues to be worried about for the Party.

Private tailors, moonlighting professional and amateur seamstresses, students and housewives—the unofficial clothes production sphere—were the first to start making jeans at home (Bartlett 2009). Fashion literature followed these home-made jeans producers and by the mid-1970s it was totally neglecting former ideological misgivings about jeans—joining efforts with the textile industry to make use of the burgeoning jeans bonanza. In a socially and sartorially somewhat

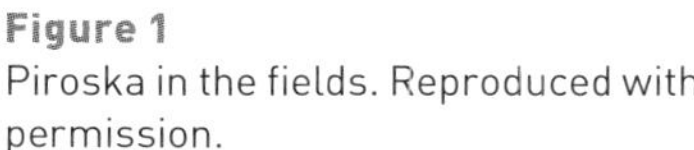
Figure 1
Piroska in the fields. Reproduced with permission.

utopian advice and educational handbook for everyday dressing, published by the Hungarian Women's Council in 1969, in the description of the items of outfit Piroska[3] wears at typical occasions in her life, her work wear for cold weather contains overalls and a pants-and-jacket set all made of "texas-vászon" (Texas canvas)—a shy and reserved early reference to jeans denim (Osvát 1969). The drawings portraying attractive fashion models posing as unskilled workers in the sugar-beet fields, wearing Hungarian-made denim jeans compress the utopian and the imaginary, resembling somewhat the unearthly promises of evangelical brochures.

First Attempts to Manufacture Jeans in Hungary

Following the early pioneers in the 1960s and early 1970s who managed to obtain jeans from abroad by traveling, or through immigrant relatives, or who could pay and were willing to pay the equivalent of a skilled worker's two-week salary for branded quality denim jeans, a mass demand for jeans started to emerge around 1974. Smaller and larger firms in the textile industry, operating in Budapest and in the country, were all eager to participate in the industry gold rush to supply customers with millions of pairs of jeans. The mid-1970s were a period of experimentation with various materials, fabrics, technologies and cuts throughout the industry. The industrial actors' strategies and performance were constrained by similar factors, all structural features of socialist planned economy: lack of independence to act in the market, lack of accessible capital to invest in know how and technology, and a low level of productivity. Manufacturers had to make money-saving compromises in the course of production, which often turned out to be detrimental to their product. József Ihász, retired textile industry manager, explained in an interview that, in the beginning, some manufacturers tried to make jeans of cotton canvas, sometimes even of mixed cotton and synthetic fiber, dyed with some kind of blue that they had at hand, which resulted in a garment that only vaguely resembled denim jeans and most importantly, did not have the desired worn look after use.

A few scattered sources have remained that document this pioneering period in jeans making. Some commentators mention certain boys' pants of the Texas,[4] Lasszó (or Hasso), and Tom Mix brands—of a grayish-bluish color and coarse to the touch, attributed to VOR (Red October Men's Clothing Factory).[5] These lacked certain jeans qualities, such as denim fabric and a jeans-style cut. *Tin trousers* (bádognadrág) was the colloquial name of a jeans product made in the mid-1970s in Karcag[6] by the May First Clothing Factory (interview with Gy. Lutor).

Vormer was another VOR jeans brand. The Szekszárd Tailors Cooperative[7] made safari-style female outfit of denim-like materials in the late 1970s and by 1978 at least ten clothing factories made some kind of jeans in Hungary. The traditional way of analyzing a garment production process, driven by notions of trademark and brand, only helps in understanding the development of this industry to a limited extent. As I will show shortly, sometimes a denim was branded and customers could buy jeans of that brand but carrying labels of different manufacturers. A branch of the May First Clothing Factory—producer of Levi's in Hungary—manufactured jeans of the Trapper brand, which was developed and branded as a cheaper but quality competitor for Levi's in Hungary.

Making Denim in Hungary

By around 1977 there seemed to be a general acknowledgement, nationwide, of the fact that jeans could not be manufactured without a durable twill-weave cotton raw material—that is, denim. It was also understood that high-quality mass production of a garment made of an unusually coarse fabric (at a competitive price) could not take place using a small-shop organization structure and traditional industry sewing machines (interview with J. Ihász). This understanding of the need for a technological upgrade did not occur overnight, though, because in the beginning leaders and professional staff in textile industry had somewhat disdainfully underestimated the difficulties of making denim.[8]

Almost simultaneously, around 1978, three major textile industry firms decided to invest in jeans manufacturing, although each chose a different strategy and these strategies determined their subsequent fate significantly.[9] The Újszeged Weaving Mill of the Hemp Spinning and Weaving Mills (HSWM)[10] had opted to make denim—including weaving, dying and sanforizing the fabric—and, except for in its final period, to

distribute the fabric widely without much attention to marketing and branding. The Buda-Flax Hungarian Linen Works[11] chose to buy indigo-dyed yarn, manufacture the fabric and to build a genuine Hungarian brand of jeans, while Buda-Flax showed little interest in garment manufacturing. May First Clothing Factory chose to make Levi's in a license agreement with Levi Strauss & Co. (LS&Co.) for export and for the national market too, using know how and materials imported to Hungary. One ought not to lose sight of the fact that, in capital-scarce socialist economies, these industry development questions were key political questions too, particularly in two respects: first, the distribution of resources to invest had been operationalized through a struggle among various industry, regional and Party lobbies, which all wanted to use scarce state funds in their own constituency. Second, firms that successfully managed the transformation of their activity into a more competitive trajectory were important examples that reformist political and technocrats' groups used, arguing that more initiative and work culture can make socialism competitive.

The Szeged-based HSWM made certain technological investments in order to move into the promising denim production field. After creating a cotton-weaving and dyeing infrastructure, by 1977 HSWM had made and sold half a million meters of denim per annum, supplying smaller and larger garment industry units all around Hungary ("Farmerhetek" 1982). The string of optimistic articles in *Hemp Industry* (*Kenderipar*), published by

the Communist Party unit in HSWM, reveal key difficulties the enterprise had to struggle with. "Our Denim's Expansion—It compares with Lee denim"—boasted the article title in 1977, but the attentive eye can discover in the text the compromises the production process had to make:

> *There are several manufacturers that make denim products in Hungary. HSWM has succeeded in making the fabric resembling the most to the original [Western jeans denim, F.H.] [...] Though the dye, of Swiss origin, used in HSWM is not identical with the original indigo dye, but it means not at all that the dye is unsatisfactory. [...] The color of HSWM-made jeans is extremely beautiful and its denim's worn look is almost the same as that of the Levi Straus[12]-made jeans.* (Csanádi 1977)

For the eye socialized in the communist period, terms such as "resembling the most," or "almost the same look" are very telling. Citizenship in communism—that is, legal and cultural norms among people, and their acknowledgement by the state—had relied heavily on the continuous official as well as non-official comparisons between East and West. The comparison of Western products with their Eastern counterparts, in most cases, and with important exceptions, had turned out to be an ordeal for the communist state. Milena Veenis (1999: 105) records her experience with former citizens of the German Democratic Republic (GDR):

> *When one asks people in East Germany to describe the power*

of attraction of Western objects, it is striking how most attempts are hampered because of the difficulty to find words for aesthetic–physical experiences. In most descriptions, people try to represent how things from the West were "somehow" softer, brighter, more colourful and cheerful [...]

As Veenis's observation may suggest, the terms "almost" or "resembling" in the self-congratulatory *Hemp Industry* article refer a core political experience in the eastern bloc; the ubiquitous "gap"—that is, the everyday material life manifestation of the Wall—between life in East and West. Another shortcoming of HSWM denim can be traced with the help of another victorious article in *Hemp Industry* from 1978. Following optimistic reports in April and May about HSWM denim's commercial success at a fair and a retail campaign ("Farmerhetek ..." 1978; "Farmerunk szép ..." 1978; Reigl 1978), *Hemp Industry* states in the title of an article in its July issue: "New Era Starts in Hungarian Jeans Manufacturing" (Makai 1978). The article, which has quite a triumphant tone, informs readers that, although HSWM's denim had ranked third after Lee and Levi's according to "certain industry literature," the firm had purchased a sanforizing system and had endeavored to produce over 1 million meters denim per annum, shrinking less than 2 percent after washing (Bérczi *et al.* 1983; Makai, 1978). From the viewpoint of fabric quality this meant that HSWM's denim had not been sanforized before.[13] Indeed, as interviewees

assert (interview with J. Ihász), non-sanforized jeans often shrank vertically and horizontally in a differing ratio, distorting the shape of the garment after washing, making jeans baggy at the knees.

Apart from dye and fabric, HSWM denim's third grave shortcoming was brand and design. As suggested by Polish, Czech, Serbian, or Slovenian terms for jeans, US jeans in postwar Eastern Europe had been connected culturally to the iconography of the Wild West much more than in the US, where the jeans had been attached rather to the subcultural bad boy image and the suburban outcast. In the late 1970s, when in the US even the drab, five-pocket Levi's had been seriously challenged by sleek designer jeans products, marketing representatives of HSWM chose to decorate the company's fair stands with a large image of a horse-riding cowboy (Reigl 1978) or with mannequins wearing jeans, dressed up in Stetsons and with lassos ("Farmerünk szép ..." 1978). HSWM's key garment manufacturer partner, Debrecen Clothing Factory, had developed a women's leisure outfit series made of HSWM denim of the Derszi[14] brand, combining, rather amusingly, allusions to safari, the Wild West, a touch of military and a generous amount of Farrah Fawcett.

In its 1978 New Year's Eve issue, *Hemp Industry* announced that, after realizing that even quality products need a brand, River Blue (1978) had been chosen as the brand of their jeans. Marketing attempts to popularize River Blue included—at just around the time of Brooke Shield's "nothing between

Figure 2
Derszi jeans from 1979. Reproduced
with permission.

my Calvin and me" controversy—
dressing up hostesses of the HSWM
stand at the Budapest International
Fair in River Blue denim blazers and
white skirts, or, in 1981, introducing
River Juliska, the puppet figure
aimed to mesmerize logo-savvy
customers (A Budapest Nemzetközi
Vásáron 1981). River Blue jeans
disappeared from written sources

and personal memories by the
mid-1980s.

Buda-Flax, an important group
of firms in flax weaving started
to make experiments in cotton
weaving in order to manufacture
denim in 1976–7. As in the case of
the HSWF in Szeged, the goal was
to make quality denim comparable
to Western jeans' fabric. Industry

experiments at several Buda-Flax
firms around the country had
included the decomposition and
thorough investigation of denim
twill in Western jeans products,
trying various raw materials and
technologies. They encountered
particular difficulties in finding
proper weft and dye for the new
denim fabric (Szénási 1988).

Unlike HSWM, which dyed the fabric, Buda-Flax, following a course of failed experiments with a sulfur-based dye as a substitute for indigo, after careful consideration chose to buy Western indigo-dyed thread instead (Kutasi 2006). Denim weaving on refurbished Western machines at the Csillaghegy firm of Buda-Flax started in late 1977 and Buda-Flax succeeded in making over 0.5 million meters of 450 g/m² denim with increasingly improving quality in 1978 and over 2 million meters in 1979 (Szénási 1988: 96). The branding of the new denim jeans, like its contemporary competitor, River Blue denim, used Wild Western iconography. Buda-Flax named the new product Trapper. Unlike HSWM in Szeged, Buda-Flax had devoted substantial resources to designing, marketing and advertising the new product, and virtually every kind of advertising

Figure 3
Trapper jeans on a museum display.
Reproduced with permission.

means (posters, magazine ads, TV and radio commercials etc.) was utilized to popularize the first Hungarian-made branded denim, which had produced certain hype around Trapper jeans. Apart from the rather appealing price of the jeans (450 HUF), the stylized Western design radically mashed with Hungarian popular cultural references (particularly with the *puszta*) all forcefully presented by the mass media, and this made an impact on customers.

In the very first period of denim production there were numerous quality problems—particularly uneven intensity of coloring of the fabric and weft snapping (Szénási 1988). While neither River Blue jeans' material features nor their fetish qualities had left noticeable traces in popular memories,[15] Trapper—although Buda-Flax suspended its production in 1992—is still a centerpiece in "socialism retro" discourses today. Trapper can be evaluated as an interesting hybrid construct half-way between a socialist garment industry product and a branded market-developed merchandise. In the production process—as testified by retired textile engineer, Csaba Kutasi—high-quality production segments were held back by connected production segments, reminding the management constantly that technological-management improvement can hardly work properly on a piecemeal basis in administratively managed socialist economies.[16] A certain duality had characterized Trapper as a brand too, because the brand's introduction to the market had shown professionally principled concerns while the brand's location in the context of Puszta Western—as something grossly un-cool—had alienated lots of customers too.[17]

Manufacturing Levi's Jeans in Marcali

In Hungarian jeans history the hot summer of 1978 brought not only big investments into weaving (at HSWM) and a full-blown advertising campaign (from Trapper) but also the opening of a garment factory in the small country town of Marcali equipped with state-of-the-art textile manufacturing technology. This would shortly produce about one million pairs of Levi's per year. The "Elegant" May First Clothing Factory (until 1952 Uniform Factory[18]) in its heyday employed about 8,000 people in several factory locations throughout the country producing men's and women's apparel. As early as around 1962–3 the May First Clothing Factory had been involved in contracted manufacturing cooperation with apparel firms based in Italy, France and the UK. Through these relations, the company had been continuously exposed to new materials and technologies, and had acquired experience of working in cooperation with capitalist firms (interview with J. Ihász).[19] In 1976, May First Clothing Factory's management decided to develop licensed cooperation with a major Western clothing manufacturer and it was decided in the same year that the garment in question would be jeans. From the first negotiations with LS&Co. about a licensed production agreement[20] in February 1977, it took only eighteen months to open the newly equipped and staffed jeans manufacturing factory on August 8, 1978. That development took place at a breathtaking business tempo by the standards of the time.

As reconstructed from interview recollections by key Hungarian participants in the Levi's project,[21] the contract prescribed very specific, often new and unusual conditions for the production and distribution of the newly manufactured product, not leaving much space for the Hungarian partner to negotiate compromises. It had been agreed that all the materials (denim, yarn, buttons, rivets, zips and tabs) for jeans would come from LS&Co.'s foreign partner companies; the May First Clothing Factory would buy the essential machinery and equipment and introduce work organization methods that LS&Co. regarded as necessary including the achievement of certain quality and productivity standards and keeping waste to a low level. It was agreed that the license fee would be covered by the May First Clothing Factory by marketable merchandise (60 percent of the output), while the rest of the merchandise was to be retailed in Hungary at a set price of 980 HUF (interviews with A. Székely and J. Ihász; Tóth 1995: 183).[22]

The key factor for understanding the nature and significance of the Levi enterprise in Hungary's economic and political history is that there was a multitude of harmonizing and conflicting motivations driving participating actors—from Marcali shop-floor assistants to Hungarian party bureaucrats or LS&Co. managers—in the course of the enterprise. Starting from the top, key motivations for the central economic policy makers (particularly the Ministry of Light Industry) had been framed in purposefully technocratic terms stressing pragmatic features on the part of the leadership. It is important to register that industry chiefs, such as Tamás Beck (President of Buda-Flax, as well as of the Hungarian Chamber of Commerce), or May First Clothing Factory CEO József Kovács were themselves powerful agents in initiating important, capital-demanding projects (interview with I. Medgyessy). As recalled by Mr József Ihász, regional director of May First Clothing Factory, the Municipal and the County Party Committees, both important players in the regional power structure, secured 3 million HUF for the Marcali project, which contribution had been framed principally in a modernization context. The media coverage of the Marcali enterprise—because of the nature of the Party-controlled media, which aimed to express the view of the Party rather than providing an unbiased news service—presented this technocratic-modernization frame with sharp contours. *Népszabadság* (*People's Freedom*), the party paper's article on the eve of the opening of the Marcali factory (Buzási 1978) praises the new enterprise mainly in terms of efficiency, accuracy and effectiveness: "Following the first spark of idea, it took only 16 months to set a contract, and only 7 months to start the production. It is a standard pace of practice in more developed European countries, while in our country it is still a sensation and an example to be followed."

The article stresses in a section with the caption "13 minutes 48 seconds" the mesmerizing industry record of the time to make a pair of jeans that the Hungarian partner would need to reach in the foreseeable future, in contrast to the standard time of 50–70 minutes in Hungary. The author seems to be particularly enthralled by the Taylorist/Fordist features of jeans production:

All the physical movements of all the workers have been developed and trained scientifically, therefore both the worker and the company benefit from the increased efficiency while the work itself would become easier [...] This [work management method] is one of the most well-organized, fastest and most efficient in the world [...] All the workers' skills with their hands and fingers had been examined with thorough methods that had served as a basis for identifying the most appropriate work and technology for each of the workers which included the setting of the machinery based on specific features of the workers. That is, not the workforce was trained for the needs of the machine, but the machine had been supplied for human needs.[23]

This last sentence from the Party paper suggests a sleek, humanist techno-utopia in a Hungarian factory making Levi's. It is very different from the late 1960s, when the same newspaper published its youth entertainment policing articles, often resulting in retaliation against individuals (Szabó 1968).

The main motivation for the May First Clothing Factory's cooperation with LS&Co. is obvious. Examples from the firm's history in international textile cooperation abound and the firm's management was aware of the significance of serving as a reference partner (behind the Iron Curtain) for LS&Co. The sheer material gain from the Levi's business played a significant role in the profit of the whole firm (interview with J. Ihász). The Marcali Levi's project linked the interests of the company and its partners in the political leadership because the LS&Co. business proved—for the political leadership and for other industrial actors—that investment in know how and technology may result in success, while in return the company and its employers were decorated with state awards.[24] As Mrs Lutor, a retired leading forewoman at the factory, recalled in an interview that I did with her, light industry minister Jánosné Keserű, at a visit to Marcali, called the Levi's factory the "jewelry box of light industry."

A variety of personal motives on the part of managers at May First Clothing Factory can be identified in the relationship with LS&Co. In an interview in 2010, Mr Ihász did not want me to write about "inferior quality" denim, even for purposes of historical research; he felt that attempts to produce jeans prior to the Levi's project were not worth investigating—that is, only quality jeans production (Levi's) is worth including in serious historical recollections.

Garment industry employers at the May First Clothing Factory's branch in Marcali—a former village that gained the municipal status

of a town in 1977—had faced an intriguingly complex set of challenges and opportunities with the opening of the jeans plant. The logic of previous garment production methods had to be completely changed based on the fact that it was difficult to increase the added value in jeans products and so shop-floor productivity had become a key factor in marketing jeans (interview with J. Ihász). LS&Co. had required the May First Clothing Factory to introduce a work organization scheme derived from the explicitly Taylorist methods-time measurement (MTM) method, called the 3M method in Hungarian.[25] Key parameters to increase efficiency in jeans making were decreasing waste and production time per product.

This highly productive work organization method challenged workers' habitual norms significantly. The work method in the jeans plant had forced workers to eliminate off-work "second shifts" at the household farm, a custom quite widespread among industrial population living in the countryside. Workers had to choose. If they wanted to keep their highly specialized jobs using state-of-the art semi-automatic machinery, they could not take on work on Monday morning with swollen, disfigured hands having spent the weekend hoeing in the family vineyard. The production line sometimes offered opportunities for women to make more money than men in similar technological positions. This reportedly sometimes created conflicts for those unable to grow accustomed to the idea that technology might change gender

Figure 4
The May First Clothing Factory's team visits the White House in January, 1978. Reproduced with permission.

positions or roles. The usual disciplinary problems in factories, common in the whole Eastern Bloc—"in-plant unemployment," absenteeism, work-time boozing, theft of products, materials and tools—were virtually unknown in the Marcali plant. The reason for the acceptance of the Marcali industry discipline was simple: the individual productivity-based salary system, making the Marcali jobs the best paid jobs in Hungarian garment industry, had proved to be a panacea for all the rigid regulations and mind-boggling monotonous work. The exceptionally high self-interest of the workers in running the plant had successfully made the workers themselves the agents of discipline, because a bottleneck caused by carelessness or idleness could jeopardize the productivity, i.e. the income, of the whole community. The production process was set by top secret documentary material[26] that Marcali managers and foreworkers could examine—without the opportunity of taking notes—only in the presence of the LS&Co. representative (a certain Mr. Roman) who resided for a longer period in Marcali.

After an initial phase, when a workforce of an appropriate size was hired by the jeans plant and the workers finished with in-house training, making Levi's models of linen canvas as practice, the plant started production and had soon yielded the 1 million pairs of Levi's per year output. In 2006, Mr Andor Székely, former Vice President of May First Clothing Factory and, according to many, the key Hungarian actor in the Levi's

Figure 5
A page from the LS&Co. documentation—nearly discarded at the liquidation of the Levi's jeans production. Reproduced with permission.

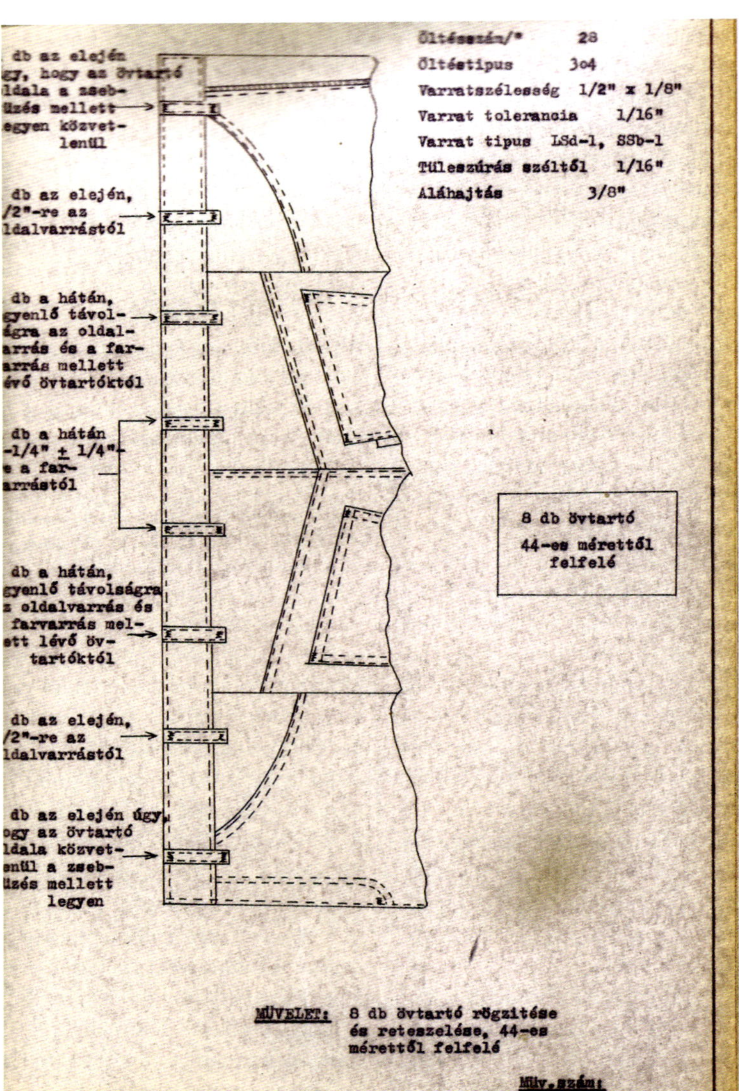

project, contended in an interview that for LS&Co. the Marcali project was a kind of adventure, resulting from curiosity about doing business behind the Iron Curtain, but the 600,000 per annum pairs of jeans the factory made for the mother company was perhaps a higher quantity than would result from something that was merely a vanity business.

The Levi plant brought a sharp change in the perception of jeans in Hungarian society. As soon after the 1978 opening in Marcali, Levi's jeans, together with its cheaper alternative, Trapper, quickly became available throughout the country. The magical status of jeans in youth culture started to fade too.[27]

Changes in jeans production in Hungary illustrated key features of Hungary's slowly opening, but structurally still non-market-driven communist economy. Driven by an obvious popular demand for millions of pairs of quality denim jeans in the 1970s, the political leadership and textile industry chiefs were able to make the necessary changes for the mass production of technology-sensitive products. The denim projects turned out to be win–win games for all the interested parties. The political leadership could express its consideration for the concerns of young people for a more stylish way of life. The jeans projects could be used as good examples of capital-sensitive industry investment in

economic modernization. Frequent bottlenecks in jeans production had proven that "islands" of modernized industries could not modify the surrounding sea of non-market-based economies, paralyzed by shortage and slack. The rough denim fabric had turned out to be a non-negotiable factor in economic policy decisions. Since indigo-dyed, sanforized, well cut and branded denim jeans just could not be substituted by cheap imitations for the customers, quality jeans had embodied non-negotiable differences between East and the West, while at the same time Hungarian-made Levi jeans or Trapper jeans held out promises—and mirages—of economic modernization.

Figure 6
Eighth-graders' party in a small town's (Dunakeszi) elementary school in 1979. All in jeans. Reproduced with permission.

Interviews

Mr Csaba Kutasi, 2010
Ms Ildikó Medgyessy, 2010
Mr József Ihász, 2010
Mr Andor Székely, 2006
Mrs Gyula Lutor, 2010
Mrs Sándor Farkas, 2010

Respondents in the "my first pair of jeans" inquiry:
Sz. Zsuzsa, b. 1968
Ny. Péter, b. 1968

Notes

1. János Kádár was the First Secretary of the Hungarian Socialist Workers' Party (HSWP) between 1956 and 1988.
2. It might seem odd but pop culture (beat music, long hair, jeans) had served as the party's iron fist against its leftist opposition because Gyurkó, as a figure of the Budapest urban intelligentsia, had been used by János Kádár and his ally Aczél in in-party struggles against the leftist conservative party opposition (personal communication with Mr. Sándor Révész).
3. The book describes the wardrobe of three ideal typical female members of Hungarian society. Piroska represents female workers in agricultural cooperatives in the countryside.
4. Texas jeans had succeeded in getting coverage from the *New York Times*: "Youths Find Link With West in 'Texas' Trousers" in which the author (Hoffman, 1968) describes the popularity of the Hungarian-made jeans.
5. Personal communication with Mr Sándor Turcsányi and Mr Zoltán Kis in 2010.
6. Ruhagyár, Karcag.
7. Szekszárdi Szabószövetkezet. It appears on a picture provided for research inspection by the Hungarian News Agency. The picture was taken on November 1, 1977.
8. Some of them had believed that Hungarian textile industries with century-long traditions could not meet the challenge of making a coarse fabric for simple five-pocket workers' pants (interview with Cs. Kutasi).
9. In a recent publication, Müller (2011) reports about a 1977 government document. In June 1977 the Ministry of Light Industries published a call for proposals for textile manufacturers to submit design projects in the fields of eight textile and leather merchandise, including jeans products. The document also indicates further (1979) government plans to fund textile enterprises that participate successfully in the 1977 bid.
10. KSZV (Kenderfonó és Szövőipar Vállalat) Újszegedi Szövőgyára.
11. Buda-Flax Lenfonó és Szövőipari Vállalat.
12. Authors of *Kenderipar* articles notoriously misspell LS&Co.'s name in highly original ways.
13. KERMI, the National Commerce Quality Control Institute, following inspection of the fabric, which included a comparison with Levi's fabric, issued its report in November 1978 about the new denim, in

which they state the HSWM's fabric is close to LS&Co.'s denim in its "character and color" (jellegben és színben közelálló) ("Jól vizsgázott …" 1978).

14. The brand Derszi is probably an acronym derived from Debreceni Ruhagyár.

15. In 2006 I placed adverts in the media to call for people's stories about their first jeans. Among the 150+ first-person recollections about "the first pair of jeans" there is only one in which the person notes, somewhat pitifully, that while he wore Trapper at the age of 10 or 11, only years later could his father manage to get his first jeans with the River Blue brand (interview with Ny. Péter, b. 1968), while dozens of stories in my collection discuss Trapper jeans in both positive and negative contexts.

16. Csaba Kutasi claims too that contemporary Trapper wearers' occasional complaints about "improper" ways of getting a faded worn look of Trapper could be caused by the fact that Trapper's fabric was unnecessarily too durable compared to branded Western jeans' fabric.

17. There is an ambivalence towards Trapper in numerous recollections. Suffice it to say that Trapper pants were regarded more highly than the marketed brand itself. Contemporary Trapper wearers report (for example in the interview with Sz. Zsuzsa, b. 1968) practices of "de-branding" Trapper jeans (removing all the tabs and labels from the jeans), which after a minimal retailoring of the legs could resemble good-quality brandless Turkish jeans from a distance.

18. Egyenruhagyár.

19. In the 1970s the May First Clothing Factory had been commissioned to perform production and management restructuring in garment manufacturing in Iraq, Mongolia, Egypt, Syria and the Soviet Union (interview with A. Székely and J. Ihász).

20. The contract appears to be lost. Generally, in license agreements, the license owner prescribes how a given product is to be produced and marketed and the license user pays in cash or in merchandise for the use of the license and sells the merchandise at a price agreed with the license owner.

21. Interviews with Mrs Farkas, Mr Ihász, Mrs Lutor and Mr Székely.

22. The price was a compromise between a reasonable Hungarian price level and the considerably higher international price of LS&Co. products (interview with J. Ihász).

23. Emphasis in original.

24. Mr Andor Székely had been awarded by the silver Order of Labor.

25. Mozdulatelemzés, munkatanulmányozás, munkakialakítás.

26. The carbon-copied A4-format booklet, called simply "the Bible" in plant lingo, had been kept in the company safe, together with photographs and further documentation. They were simply discarded after the discontinuation of the Marcali Levi production in 1988 but were saved by an attentive worker.

27. After 1985 Wrangler jeans were retailed by Interfer Co. in Hungary (Méri 2006).

References

"A Budapesti Nemzetközi Vásáron." 1981. *Kenderipar* 23 (September 30): 2.

Bartlett, Djurdja. 2009. "Ideológia és viselet." In Ildikó Simonovits and Tibor Valuch (eds) *Öltöztessük fel az országot! Divat és öltözködés a szocializmusban*. Budapest: Argumentum Kiadó, Budapesti Történeti Múzeum, 1956-os Intézet.

Bérczi, I., Kónya, S. and Markovits, T. 1983 *A Kenderfonó és Szövőipari Vállalat 20 éve. Szeged 1963–1983*. Szeged: Kenderfonó és Szövőipari Vállalat.

"Blue River." 1978. *Kenderipar* 20 (December 31): 7.

Buzási, J. 1978. "Márkás farmer Marcaliból." *Népszabadság* (August 6): 4.

Csanádi, E. 1977. "Farmeranyagunk térhódítása—Vetekszik az eredeti Lee-vel." *Kenderipar* 19 (September 17): 13.

Csillik, András. 1971. "Válasz Gyurkó Lászlónak." *Valóság* (August): 127–8.

Deés, Enikő. 1972. *Divatról fiataloknak*. Budapest: Minerva.

"Farmerhetek a szegedi Centrum Áruházban." 1978. *Kenderipar* 20 (May 27): 6.

"Farmerunk szép sikere." 1978. *Kenderipar* 20 (June 10): 2.

Gyurkó, László. 1971. "Nyílt levél a KISZ Központi Bizottságához." *Valóság*, pp. 72–3.

Hammer, Ferenc. 2008. "Sartorial Manoeuvres in the Dusk: Blue Jeans in Socialist Hungary." In Frank Trentmann and Kate Soper (eds) *Citizenship and Consumption*, pp. 51–68. Basingstoke: Palgrave Macmillan.

Hoffman, Paul. 1968. "Blue Jeans Mark Trend in Hungary." *New York Times,* August 4, p. 3, http://select.nytimes.com/gst/abstract.html?res=F10B11FD3E5C1A7B93C6A91783D85F4C8685F9 (accessed December 29, 2010).

"Jól vizsgázott farmeranyagunk." 1978. *Kenderipar* 20 (November 29): 1.

Kutasi Csaba. 2006. "A Trapper farmer és a többiek." *Textil Fórum* 16(336): 6–7.

Makai, Ildikó. 1978. "Új szakasz kezdődik a magyar farmergyártásban." *Kenderipar* 20 (July 27): 5.

Méri, Edina. 2006. *Az örökéletű farmer.* Pápa: Kékfestő Múzeum.

Müller, Fruzsina. 2011. "Farmerprogram. A farmerhiány megszüntetése: a szocialista Magyarországon." *Múltunk* 56(4): forthcoming.

Osvát, Katalin (ed.). 1969. *Tetőtől talpig.* Budapest: Magyar Nők Országos Tanácsa, pp. 47–58.

Reigl, Endre. 1978. "Pannónia Vásár Szabadkán." *Kenderipar* 20 (April 27): 1.

Szabó, Ferenc. 1968. "Egy este az Eötvös Klubban." *Népszabadság* (January 19).

Szénási, Éva. 1988. *Buda-Flax Csillaghegyi Szövőgyárának története: 1925–1985.* Budakalász: Buda-Flax Lenfonó és Szövőipari Vállalat.

Tóth, László. 1995. "Textiles/Garments: Elegant Charm." In Saul Estrin *et al.* (eds.) *Restructuring and Privatization in Central Eastern Europe: Case Studies of Firms in Transition (Microeconomics of Transition Economies).* Armok, NY: Sharpe, Inc.

Veenis, Milena. 1999. "Consumption in East Germany. The Seduction and Betrayal of Things." *Journal of Material Culture* 4(1): 79–122.

Making New Vintage Jeans in Japan: Relocating Authenticity

Abstract

Japan has become renowned as a site for the production of artisanal-quality denim and jeans, which appeals to increasingly discerning cognoscenti. The usual mass-produced, non-designer "safe" denim has a ubiquitous presence in Japan as it does elsewhere but there are many Japanese for whom a pair of jeans has many more qualities that should be carefully considered before its consumption than the perhaps usual factors of price, brand, cut, wash and color. These include the types of machines the denim was woven on, the presence of certain (sometimes invisible) rivets, the technique of stitching and so on. "Made in Japan" has become the catchphrase for new denim authenticity sought by "denim maniacs" (*denimu mania no hito*). This paper gives a brief history of jeans in Japan, introduces the area where they are made and examines two jeans companies as well as consumers of these premium jeans. It looks at how expensive Japanese jeans echo the *mingei* craft movement in their emphasis on method of production over the aesthetics of the final product. It shows that authenticity in Japan can be relocated both geographically and from the "original" to the "copy."

Keywords: denim, Japan, authenticity, vintage, copying

PHILOMENA KEET

Philomena Keet carried out this research while a Hosei International Fund scholar at Hosei University, Tokyo. Her social anthropology PhD research (SOAS, University of London) is about a youth fashion scene in Tokyo.

Textile, Volume 9, Issue 1, pp. 44–61
DOI: 10.2752/175183511X12949158771437
Reprints available directly from the Publishers.
Photocopying permitted by licence only.

Making New Vintage Jeans in Japan: Relocating Authenticity

Introduction—Making Jeans, Rendering Authenticity

This paper will look at the production and consumption of premium "vintage" denim in Japan, arguing that high-end Japanese jeans, through various production and marketing strategies, resolve the "authenticity anxiety" (Taylor Atkins 2000: 31) of trying to be authentic Japanese individuals through an originally American cultural product. This has had a rather peculiar consequence of more general interest to those following the trajectories of contemporary denim. These local issues have led to a broader shift in the geographical authenticity of "new" vintage jeans away from America to Japan, such that even American jeans brands, for example cult brand PRPS, stake their claim to "being real" partly through the use of Japanese denim.[1] While this seems to go against notions of authenticity being concerned with origins, it seems odd that one country can effectively appropriate the forms of authenticity for another. These Japanese jeans also show how authenticity can be perceived differently between and within cultures.

Much of this research was carried out during the summer and autumn of 2009 during two stays in the town of Kojima in west Japan, which is known as the locus for artisanal production of denim, as well as through related national magazines and jeans shops in Tokyo. In Kojima I interviewed staff at shops-cum-showrooms and various jeans-related factories.[2] While considering the connoisseur consumer, this paper is therefore biased towards the producers of denim and jeans for the purpose of investigating how Japanese denim products are rendered as authentic through manufacturing processes, sales talk and advertising. As Moeran (1997) found with the pottery produced in rural Japan, the physicality of the final jeans product was not always as important as the mechanisms by which it was created. I will argue that this is true for the jeans described in this paper and will focus on the manufacturing processes and how the final jeans product is planned in two Kojima-based companies.

Following the idea that authenticity is socially constructed (Peterson 1997) and not inherent to an object, I will look at how denim production companies in Japan have been successful at "rendering authenticity" (Gilmore and Pine 2007) through such authenticating strategies (Taylor Atkins 2000) as employing old machines no longer used in America and now-defunct time-consuming techniques. Premium or high-end jeans are characterized variously by being high-quality denim, better fitting, produced on a small scale and designer-led and retail for over US$100 a pair (sometimes much more). Within this, there is a category of vintage reproduction jeans that are not judged so much on objective quality but by factors such as stitch color and the presence of "hidden rivets." The popularity of vintage jeans is part of a larger trend in Japan's oversaturated markets for making consumption decisions on the basis of the opportunities a commodity presents for achieving personal authenticity (Lindholme 2008).

Authenticity belongs to the "set of values that includes sincere, essential, natural, original, and real" (Lindholme 2008: 1) and as such is defined against what is fake, replica, copy, artificial. While the authentic holds a true and real relationship to some origin and/or content (it is what it "purports to be" Lindholme 2008: 2) the degree to which these correspondences are significant may differ between cultures, giving rise to variation in what is considered to be authentic. In particular, cultures that have historically very different philosophical backgrounds to that in the "West" may conceive of "authenticity" somewhat differently. Vann (2006) found, for example, that fake and genuine goods in Vietnam were classified in a way that did not fit with international intellectual property laws. Hendry suggests that in Japan, authenticity lies not only in a unitary correspondence to the "real thing" (*honmono*) but can also be experienced through faithful replication (2000). This is crucial in understanding how Japanese replicas of American vintage jeans have become highly sought after, not only in Japan but throughout the world.

Japan has become a new locale of authenticity for denim but what does authenticity mean in the case of denim? Jeans are inextricably associated with America (despite the fact that the denim material and name "jeans" both originate in Europe). Levi's 501xx vintage models attract the highest premiums, and the older the better.[3] The 501 style,[4] still in production today, has the longest history of any jeans cut in the world. Although there have been changes over the century or so since it first came into existence, it remains the model of genealogical authenticity for any denim lover.[5] When searching for the most authentic newly produced jeans (which is necessary due to the rarity of such vintage pairs), however, Japanese denim fans choose these "super jeans" (Izuishi 1999: 244)[6] that are assembled in Japan using denim woven in Japan over their American counterparts. I will look at how certain Japanese jeans companies come to portray themselves as, and be seen as, more or less authentic than others, particularly with respect to the "original" American brands. As I will argue, there is also a move towards greater personal authenticity such that jeans are made for maximum "fit" to the wearer as well as being rendered as genealogically or correspondently authentic. First I will look at the history of jeans in Japan, and how the domestication of American jeans led eventually to the production of authentic Japanese "super denim."

History of Japanese Denim

The first jeans available for purchase in Japan were second-hand jeans obtained from the American occupation forces, to be found first in Kobe and Tokyo's Ueno around 1946. Known as "G.I. pants" (*ji-ai pantsu*), they were abbreviated to "*G-pan*": jeans are still known by this moniker in present day Japan. Being second hand, they were soft and worn, but invariably available in sizes that were too big for many of the young people who hankered after them. The charismatic founder of Japanese jeans brand Evisu, Yamane, tells a story of his first experience trying to get hold of a pair of these *G-pan*. As a young middle-school boy he wondered what *G-pan* meant: "I'll never forget the shop assistant saying 'It means G.I. pants.' Those words sent shivers down my spine" (Yamane 2008: 30).

Jeans therefore made a somewhat eventful entrance to Japan: they were not thought of as fashionable but rather represented a worn, hardy, work-wear type of anti-fashion or *jitsuyouhin* (literally "utility goods"). However, at the same time, having been actually worn by these G.I.s, they came infused with all the mixed feelings of resentment and exoticism towards these American occupants. It was perhaps this streak of "the enemy" in the very fabric of the *G-pan* that was so affecting to Yamane and others.

While *G-pan* were available from the beginning of the Occupation era, it was not until the mid-1960s that Japan really started to produce its own denim. The background to this development is a confluence of geography, population and industrial changes, factors that all came together with a particular company, Maruo (Sugiyama 2009). Based in the small town of Kojima in the prefecture of Okayama, West Japan, the company, later known as Big John, was one of many in the region that were producing school uniforms, but the first to switch to making jeans. On finally producing their first pairs, they had trouble selling them: Japanese customers would not buy such starchy and stiff trousers.[7] They started to pre-wash the jeans; Japan was therefore one of the first countries in which denim washing processes developed. Other companies started to follow Big John, including their main, and now far more successful, rivals— Edwin. Edwin managed to gain the rights to sell Levi's and Lee in Japan, and thus the Japan jeans market expanded rapidly in the 1970s and 1980s. Japan started to make its own machines for the industrial weaving and stitching of denim.

Up until the 1990s, most jeans that were made in Japan played down their origin and used marketing and production strategies that affiliated them with America, almost masquerading as American brands. Indeed Edwin (supposedly named "Edo-win" as a

Figure 1
The uniform industry is still a presence in Kojima.

challenge to their west Japan rivals) has frequently used Brad Pitt in its advertising and was commonly thought of as an American brand. Big John was well known for being the first Japanese denim brand but with such a name the cultural references are obvious.

Starting in the 1980s but continuing into the 1990s, the burgeoning denim scene in Japan led to a quest by both producers and consumers to find a "better," more authentic pair of jeans from amongst the variety and quantity of denim being produced. "The early 1990s saw jeans spread as everyday wear, but it was also a period in which the value of old jeans that used to be worn as work wear was re-established," states the website of the Japan Jeans Association (www.best-jeans. com, accessed December 2009). Pairs of vintage Levi's were sought out and brought back to Japan from thrift shops in America and Europe and were scientifically and systematically analyzed. The threads were unraveled and subject to tests that revealed their thickness, density and other physical properties. The discrepancies between the lettering on the rivets, the back patches, the stitching and so on of different years were carefully documented and recorded. Eventually guides were produced that would allow one to date a vintage pair of Levi's to a particular year.

At this point the locus of the "real thing" was very firmly placed in these old American Levi's, and many of them were bought

Figure 2
One of the publications which documents how the features of vintage Levi's changed year by year.

by denim companies eager to discover and replicate the qualities by which they were so highly evaluated. Studio D'artisan made if not the first then one of the first pairs of "vintage jeans," their D01 model. A pamphlet produced for their 30th anniversary in 2009 describes them as "the antithesis of the rationalism always sought by the motherland" (Lightning 2009a: 27), pointing to the craftsmanship and tradition that the company had learnt from Europe. Years after the more niche Studio D'artisan, mainstream brand, Edwin came out with the oxymoronically named "New Vintage" range in 1994. Natural indigo was reintroduced because chemical indigo dyes did not produce the fading that was a mark of vintage jeans (Taussig 2008).

The history of jeans in Japan seems to illustrate perfectly the image of Japan as nation that copies, domesticates and improves (Cox 2008; Taylor Atkins 2000; Tobin 1992). There is a hint in these accounts that Japan falls short in innovation, which is as mistaken for jeans as it is for the Sony Walkman (Du Gay *et al.* 1997). Japan was an innovator of denim distressing techniques and washing in particular (Sugiyama 2009). In the Studio D'artisan brochure, it says of the 1980s that "people appeared who were trying things out that couldn't be done in the motherland, America" (Lightning 2009a: 27). It is because emerging jeans brands were able to combine innovative Japanese know-how with what they had learnt about "original" vintage denim that they could forge for themselves a "new authenticity."

Kojima as Authenticating Strategy

The town of Kojima has become an important authenticating strategy in itself for many of these premium Japanese denim brands. It is written about in tourist literature and denim promotional material as the "birthplace" of jeans (*ji-nzu no hassyouchi*). Tourism within Japan is strongly linked to regional specialties and souvenirs and, like the rice spoons (*shamoji*) of Miyajima (Daniels 2001), denim gains a certain spirituality from its association with Kojima, spreading the "fame" of Kojima as it is consumed throughout the country. "The place where D'artisan jeans are born, the denim Mecca Kojima" runs one headline in a pamphlet. The national train company, JR West, produces a pamphlet about a "jeans bus" that takes denim tourists around Kojima's showrooms, museums and shops. Television programs see celebrities traveling to Kojima to get a pair of order-made jeans that they distress themselves. There is much truth in this image: Kojima is a place whose extensive network of small enterprises that grew around its uniform production industry, specializing in sewing, fasteners and so on, lent themselves well to the production of denim (Sugiyama 2009). The small size of the enterprises (there was a saying that in Kojima you could throw a stone and hit a company president), and the well-connected network they formed meant that about ten years ago it was easy for small, innovative makers to conduct their own jeans experiments. It certainly formed the nucleus of independent jeans production in particular. Kojima is romanticized as the location of these special old shuttle looms, the place where *aizome* (dyeing from Japanese indigo plants) craftsmen (*shokunin*) work and so on. While this was true a decade or so ago, the town's current situation reveals a somewhat different picture.

The jeans bus is a regular bus that follows the normal route with images of jeans daubed on its sides. The Betty Smith Jeans Museum is closed by default but, on the rare occasion a visitor arrives, a lady rushes across to unlock the door and switch on the lights and video presentations. The most popular attraction in Kojima remains the old house of the salt pioneer, Nozaki. There are old looms in Kojima but even jeans that are assembled and/or washed and distressed there usually get their denim material from Fukuyama, further West. There are some more senior craftsmen remaining, but for the most part "super jeans" are more likely to be sewn up in a small factory staffed by young Chinese women workers. Production sites are closing down all the time. Like the Onta potters (Moeran 1997) who are propelled towards more individually based modes of production despite their show of solidarity, the Kojima image of craft locale is at odds with its current situation in which the network of smaller producers is breaking down and giving way to larger companies that take manufacturing orders as well as having their own brands. Kojima is a somewhat lackluster jeans Mecca, but for the super denim cognoscenti it remains an important signifier of quality.[8] This authentically rendered image of Kojima has helped to relocate some of the jeans authenticity of America to this other "birthplace."

Two Kojima Jeans Makers

There are dozens of "super jeans" companies who specialize in "Made in Japan" new vintage denim, many of whom are based in Kojima, such as Momotaro Jeans. These makers are regularly listed in book-style magazines that are published perhaps on a yearly basis as special editions, like the Lightning magazine series of "denim books" (for example, Lightning 2009b). I will look at one of the key "super jeans" companies, Studio D'artisan, hereafter shortened to D'artisan but known affectionately by its fans as D'arti (*daruchi*). The firm is based in Osaka, but the factory where all the washing and distressing is done is in Kojima. I will compare the authenticating strategies used by D'artisan with those of another very small maker, Tuki, based in Okayama not far from Kojima. Both are concerned only with making what they regard to be the best products they can, without pandering to the demands of their customer base. This is an authenticating discourse that distances the companies from profit

Figure 3
A jeans sewing (*hosei*) factory in Kojima, operated by a roomful of young women from China, not the image of a solitary old craftsman that is often portrayed.

motives and from making their discerning customers from feeling like they are being "sold to." While both brands are concerned with achieving a certain authenticity, the form that authenticity takes and the strategies used to render it are very different, showing how denim/jeans authenticity is multivalent and possible to render in a number of ways.

Studio D'artisan

Studio D'artisan was founded early in the history of Japanese denim in 1969 from a desire to reproduce vintage denim using Japanese materials and techniques, including the *aizome* indigo dyeing that had flourished in Japan for centuries. The man who started it, Takagi, was studying abroad in Europe where he would forage in local bazaars and markets for old jeans and military garb. There are suggestions that Takagi was the first to think of making reproduction vintage jeans that matched the classics in shape and texture. "He's the one that came up with it all," said Mr. Fujiwara, the current president of the company. The French name, translating as "craftsman's studio" encapsulates an idea held of a European craftsman, operating separately and less commercially than his American jeans industry counterpart. Now, D'artisan's core customers range from 18 to 60 years old, with some of the older clientele having patronized the brand for much of its history. Most D'artisan jeans are just under 20,000 yen, roughly US$200, with many costing significantly more, especially if they have been subject to washing and other "processing" (*kakou*).

"Now, vintage jeans are accepted without question, but at the time [thirty years ago] it was only D'artisan who were focusing on *aizome* dyeing and who took up jeans in a real (*honkakuteki*) way" states D'artisan's thirtieth anniversary booklet (Lightning 2009a: 26). But there is a clear paradox here. How can you newly "make" vintage? Why is not called, more accurately "reproduction" vintage? Second-hand vintage Levi's are distinguished by calling them *furugi*, literally old clothes. "Vintage refers to the type of material—it's the narrow-width fabric" explains Fujiwara. By making the denim fabric on old shuttle looms similar to the ones that produced the original jeans of the early twentieth century (in many cases on the very same looms used over fifty years ago), "vintage-ness," a key element of authenticity, can be literally woven into the new jeans. In a slight departure from the loss of aura via mechanical reproduction (Benjamin 1992), the "vintage" aura of these jeans has been reinstated through production techniques, which though mechanical, are sufficiently outdated to pass as "original." Hendry (2000) finds the same creation of authenticity can be achieved by using the same methods to make a new copy that were used to make an old original in the case of a replica of Shakespeare's house that was built for a theme park in Japan. The replica was, she argued, more authentic than the original old house since it was a faithful copy that furthermore was unsullied by the passage of time. The same can be said for D'artisan jeans.

Weaving denim from old shuttle looms rather than modern projectile ones not only takes more time to produce a length of a narrower width fabric but it leaves a characteristic edge that is not frayed, called "selvedge."[9] This selvedge denim is one of the strategies used by not only D'artisan, but by many of these smaller companies and more recently, following Japan's lead, by global high-fashion brands, in the rendering of historical authenticity. However, the majority of D'artisan jeans are not made from such selvedge denim, getting their denim instead from Fukuyama: in fact only the SP-006 selvedge model is advertised as a "Made in Kojima" model. So what of all the other non-selvedge D'artisan jeans? How do they come to bear the patina of authenticity? D'artisan jeans have features that are literally copied from vintage models: the width of the belt loops, the color of the stitching (also done on old machines), even the leather patch features two pigs (the D'artisan logo) pulling apart a pair of jeans, in a blatant homage to Levi's two horses. The sales techniques of the shop assistants in the D'artisan shops emphasize these features. As Fujiwara explained: "The staff take time to explain the difference between the various jeans to customers. Whether it's one- or non-wash, how it was woven, how it was stitched, how it was dyed, how the jeans will change once you wear them, whether they'll shrink after you wash them or not …" While calling to attention the high "craftsmanship" that goes into producing D'artisan jeans, the sales patter also incorporates the

concept that the jeans must not only be authentic in themselves but authentic to the wearer, the customer. Do they suit not only your body shape, but your overall appearance and *funiki* (atmosphere, aura)? Like all of these strategies, this is not unique to D'artisan and some brands claim to go so far as to actually dissuade customers from buying their jeans if a fitting proves less than satisfactory. This stems from the same refusal to be seen to be interested in profit at the expense of craft and quality. "Our stance is just to make good things and have them recognized by our customers" said Fujiwara, denying they have a market whose tastes they actively target.

This rationale echoes the ideal of *chokkan* (direct perception) that was central to Yanagi's concept of *mingei* (folk art) (Moeran 1997). It implies a universal aesthetic that if the self is subsumed, can be recognized as "good" or "beautiful" by anybody. Moeran shows however that this *chokkan* is not achieved in practice and that there is no inherent aesthetic standard in these jeans but a set of values that derive from recreating the features, and importantly, by the same methods (the old shuttle loom for example) as early "original" jeans.

Denim is perhaps unique in being the only fabric whose resultant garments we are happy to buy when they show obvious signs of wear and tear (Miller and Woodward 2007). On a visit to the shop in Tokyo and later the factory in Kojima, D'artisan's president was always most animated when excitedly showing me the qualities of these particular jeans. He

presents them to me, exclaiming: "These are new (*shinpin*)." This is indeed surprising as not only were they faded and worn, as is common for pre-distressed jeans, but they were also incredibly soft and malleable. An attempt to stand them up resulted in the waist concertinaing into the frayed ankles with barely any starchy resistance. "We process them until the point that they would rip if we did it anymore" says Fujiwara. Indeed there are no holes in the main body of the denim, although the bottoms were frayed, and a semicircle was completely worn away at the heel as if someone had been walking around for years in these jeans, which were too long for them. He was clearly very proud of this achievement and would not reveal all of the methods he used to get them so soft.[10] "These don't just look like vintage jeans," he said, "they feel like them." These jeans cost a good couple of hundred dollars more for the privilege of having them not just aesthetically, but texturally processed to a mock pre-worn state. Jeans in their "original" state, as work wear (*jitsuyouhin*), demanded the presence of being faded, frayed and torn. As a result of the softness of vintage Levi's, softness became a marker of authenticity in itself that has been pursued to extremes here. D'artisan have produced by mechanical means denim that not only looks like its historical precedent but feels probably softer than any vintage jeans would have done through merely wearing them, working in them and washing them for years.

This pair of new jeans has been subject to various processes all

Figure 4
New (*shinpin*) vintage reproduces
wear-and-tear particularly faithfully.

taking time and money in their execution and development in order to look and feel as much like a pair of original, early twentieth-century jeans in their *jitsuyouhin* worn state. That is, their authentic value derives from their particularly faithful visual and tactile reproduction of an original, not in their genealogical or essential relationship to the original itself. Like the Shakespeare house, in fact, they are better than the original, precisely because they come in the state of being soft and worn-in, something that the original can only achieve through the passage of time. The great enthusiasm that continues amongst Japanese denim enthusiasts for vintage Levi's 501xx shows that the original remains highly privileged as a locus of authenticity in Japan, but when they cost over a thousand dollars, a pair of pre-worn jeans made using similar techniques and with a similar aesthetic satisfies the desire for authenticity at a lower cost.

Tuki

Kosuke Harada and his wife are the pair behind the brand Tuki. Rather than a denim brand exclusively, it makes various trousers, or *pantsu*, but their main product is jeans. As a student of literature at university, Harada loved denim and looking back, refers to himself at that time as a *denimu maniakku* (a serious denim fan). As was common in Japan in the 1990s at the start of the vintage boom, he use to spend literally thousands of dollars on vintage denim, seeking out the rarer older Levi's and comparing how they felt to wear in comparison with other vintage jeans. He set up on his own after working for six years as a planner in a large, high fashion jeans and clothes maker also based in Kojima, which is where he met his wife who was designing there.

The almost obsessive interest in denim that Harada held when he was a student, and his experiments in "comparative wearing" (*hakikuraberu*), have left him with a scientific approach to his denim, the potential of which is fully realized in his "denim research laboratory" (*denimu kenkyuujyo*). Housed in a large room in an institution to support start-up businesses funded by Okayama prefecture, the pair sit surrounded by patterns, sewing machines, new jeans and old jeans that look like they have been dissected. In fact as part of his research into what makes a pair of jeans "good," Harada spent months reducing part of a pair of 1947 Levi's 501xx vintage jeans (that would be worth about $1500 now) into its constituent parts. Unraveling the strands that are woven together to form the denim material, he then painstakingly teased apart those strands, until the jeans became nothing more than a series of threads in different clear pots. Somehow he had even managed to produce cotton balls from the threads. These are then sent off to be analyzed by special machines owned by larger companies. Harada operates as if he is trying to discover the scientific formula behind vintage Levi's 501xx. This reduction and analysis was common in denim companies, hence the presence of such specialist machines, but they also constitute trade secrets, so Harada is finding out thread thickness, weight and so on for himself.

Whereas D'artisan authenticating strategies tend to work by connecting newly manufactured jeans with notions of jeans "in the good old days" (*furukiyoki*, literally "good old," appears frequently in the D'artisan promotional material) and with ideals of high-quality craftsmanship, the authenticating strategies employed by Tuki take a very different route. Harada is dismissive of their recourse to "the good old days," bemoaning that "stories" play too large a part in both marketing jeans, and in consumption choices. He implies, that regardless of the inherent qualities of the garment in question, its value is determined largely by these authenticating "stories," which form the core of the exercise of branding. In D'artisan's case these include "stories" about the old shuttle looms used to weave some of their denim; of D'artisan's founding roots combining Takagi's passion for denim with his European experiences; of highly skilled *aizome* craftsmen. Harada has little regard for such stories, and taking their place are his concerns with "objective" physical and tactile excellence, hence his denim analysis exercises. Although he has chosen an old vintage Levi's pair of jeans as his model of best feel and quality, thereby seemingly harking back to the same old "origin stories" of other brands, his student period of "comparative wearing" formed a kind of experimental method by which he refined his denim evaluation and arrived at this pair. Again the *mingei* ideal of *chokkan* surfaces here in a more convincing form than

Figure 5
A pair of 1947 Levi's is dissected and subjected to analysis.

in the Onta pots and D'arti jeans because the physical qualities of the product are considered more important than the methods used to achieve them. Moeran (1997) describes how potters themselves could not tell the difference between pots thrown on kick and mechanical wheels but that, for critics and consumers, how the pottery is made is more important than what it was because the method of production stood for a community relationship of solidarity.

Rather than employing strategies of production and marketing that imbue his products with the aura of the authentic original, he instead appeals to an authenticity of content, of essence. What Harada is seeking to achieve is a paring down to the simplest model of the ideal jeans form, which gains its value not from historicity but from objectively investigated qualities. This paring down is a quest for authenticity of a kind of jeans core, the authenticity of the essential shape and texture, regardless of geographical or historical background. It shows how, even within Japan, even within an industry, authenticity can be rendered differently.

Harada is now producing a black label, "which is minus, minus, minus." He strips away any surplus features, unnecessary historically authenticating elements, chiseling away to reveal his idea of the authentic, real essence of quality jeans. He does not use selvedge denim, suspicious of the claims of superior quality and avoiding recourse to such "stories." "Selvedge is just a fad," he says. The label on the back of the jeans is not supersized—it is black leather

and features no mark of any kind. Again, the leather label is present as an element of the prototypical real jean but it does away with the tan leather color of the label associated with "vintage" jeans, replacing it with the non-color black, and with no logo or text. This is minimalism, an aesthetic often associated with Japan, taken to an extreme, echoing the *mingei* qualities of removing any decoration to focus purely on function.

His marketing style is similarly minimal: he not only refrains from advertising his brand but refuses to appear in the special-issue denim magazines that showcase D'artisan and other small-scale, premium brands not dissimilar from Tuki. All that is left is word of mouth. "I just make very particular things (*kodawatteiru mono wo tsukuru*). If they are *really* stylish, they'll just spread (*yoppodo kakkou yokatara, tysuuyou suru*). All I want is for people to think 'this is nice'." This echoes D'artisan's ethos of just making good products, and trusting that customers will follow, although the kind of customers he has in mind are different from D'artisan's typical customers, who will be described more below.

What is the attraction to customers of these simple, honed jeans "prototypes," with no extra rivets, special color stitching, label decoration and so on?

Despite Harada's opinions on the matter, Tuki also has a story: it is one concerning the pure, the essential, the stripped-down, the "real," the unadulterated. It is the jeans equivalent of a blank canvas and so it allows maximum ownership by the consumer, the wearer. When you buy a pair of D'artisan new "vintage" jeans, their processing in industrial washing machines allowing one to feel that you have been wearing them for years the instant you put them on—you are forestalling the possibility of those jeans wearing in a way that is truly unique to your body. There are no pre-rubbed crease marks (*hige*) on Tuki jeans: any crease marks that develop will be of your own body's making, any fading of the denim color will be as a result of how and when you choose to wash them. While D'artisan's rendering of authenticity locates the "real" outside of the wearer's corporality and self, Tuki moves the real closer to the individual. Of course, in their own ways these are both strategies, stories: on the one hand, the products of both brands are as manufactured and "fake" as the other; on the other, they stories render them just as real and authentic to the wearers. The main difference is where the stories locate the origins, the reality, to which the authenticity harks.

Denim Fans—Satisfying Your Self

So far I have considered how jeans producers attempt to render authenticity in their products. They claim that they do not target particular markets but it is clear from their continued existence that there is a market for these authentically rendered jeans. Who comprises this market, and why, if they are spending an average of US$200 plus on jeans, do they not choose to spend the same amount on more widely recognized and status-bestowing high-fashion designer jeans?

I first came across the term *denimu maniakku* when talking to an employee of Kojima-based premium denim maker Nola, named Nakajima. He was telling me about his company's jeans, which are not dissimilar in many ways to D'artisan's (and the large majority of other small makers that feature in the same denim special issues). Giving me what was surely a version of his sales patter, he proudly showed me the old machine that they used for the stitching, on display in their Kojima shop-cum-showroom. He explained that only jeans stitched on such old machines acquired real diagonal "puckering" on the hems. Continuing with the "authentic" features of the jeans, he told me to press down on the area around the pocket, pointing out the presence of rivets that, despite being invisible, were significant in their mere presence. What kind of person would be impressed by an invisible feature?[11] Who would care about puckering, which is not a feature that makes the jeans any better to wear, or necessarily better to look at? *Mania no hito* was the answer: obsessive fans, cognoscenti, or denim "geeks" (*otaku*). Not wishing to make them sound as if they are slightly unhinged, I will refer to them as fans, not maniacs (as would be the literal translation), although the term *maniakku* includes the elements both of strong liking for jeans (fans) and deep knowledge about them (cognoscenti).

The shop assistant himself admitted to being such a fan. "Us mutual fans (*mania doushi*) will look back at each other's jeans if we pass in the street" he says. "If

often happens to me." These fans can identify a pair of these "super jeans" at a mere glance from factors such as the fabric quality and color, the presence of selvedge, the fit, distressing patterns and of course the labels and back-pocket stitching.

On the day I met him, Nakajima was wearing a pair of jeans that were a loose, wide fit. The denim was crisp, starchy, a deep blue and had a slight surface sheen. The hems were turned up and the selvedge on display. There was no red thread: "we use beige thread, it's more natural." I asked how long he had been wearing that pair. "Since April 1" he replied, with unexpected precision. Nakajima, like his fellow denim fans, treats the wearing of jeans with as much interest and care as they do their selection for purchase.

I have been wearing them every day since then, and haven't washed them yet. The last pair I wore for 11 months without washing, but then my baby threw up on them so I had to. I stopped wearing them then. I still have them, folded up and put away. I wanted to wear them for a year precisely, as I did with the pair prior to that. I plan to wear them again at some point in the future.

The point of wearing each identical pair for a fixed period of time was that they ended up with a shape, wear, color and feel that were all "unique to yourself" (*jibun senyou*). "Your face (*kao*) comes out through them" he added. With one pair he experimented by washing them every three months, in order to compare them with a pair that was not washed at all.

It is not only how often you wear and wash your jeans that is of concern to the denim fan but also how you wash them. The Lightning "Denim Book" guide (2009) has a few pages at the front where they ask denim fans: "What brand denim are you wearing? What do you like about them? How long have you been wearing them? How often do you wear them? How do you wash them?" The answers to the last question include "I don't; normally; with special denim wash; and water only."

Studio D'artisan is one of the best-known brands that attracts these denim fans. When it opened its first shop in Tokyo, a queue of fans had formed outside. People had come from as far as Japan's northern island, Hokkaido. There is at least one D'artisan customer who owns over a hundred pairs, according to the president. "These denim fans are a small slice of the pie. There are fewer and fewer people who think 'If it's not like this, it's no good.'" One of the biggest consumer stories of 2009 in Japan was the rise of ultra-cheap (*gekiyasu*) jeans, meaning under around US$10. But the consensus seems to be that if these small makers can keep their core customers of *denim maniakku*, then their continuation and that of Kojima will be possible.

The main demographic of these "Made in Japan" premium jeans are men over thirty-five years of age: they have both the disposable income to treat themselves to a pair of jeans that will last and they have passed the adolescent and young adult periods of experimenting with and being interested in changing fashions. A stance that many of

these jeans makers take is that they are not in the "fashion" business. They seem to say that whereas fashion is volatile and superficial, their products are perceived as historically grounded, stable and "real." Harada, once more, does not hold this attitude: just as he is not interested in linking his jeans to an authentic past, he does not see his products as separate from fashion. There is a timelessness, a constancy about this conception of authenticity. He reasons that there are two types of people who are interested in vintage jeans and their new repro-counterparts: teenagers and young adults, and men approaching middle age and over. The former category research, buy and wear these jeans as part of the larger project of finding themselves as Harada did when he was a university student; the latter category choose their jeans and wear them as a result of having graduated from this youthful process and having settled into their own style. A more negative view would hold that these are another breed of *otaku* who wear these repro-vintage jeans because they have no confidence in participating in "fashion." Rather than spending money on an expensive pair of jeans that mark them out as being "of the moment," they spend money on a pair that gives them the satisfaction of having the best craftsmanship quality and something that is as close to the "real thing" as they can get. The purchase and wearing results in "self satisfaction" (*jiko manzoku*) as Nakajima put it. Brands like D'artisan and Tuki are barely known except outside these fan circles, so if there are status symbols at all it is only to the wearer. The search for the *honkaku-teki* pair of "super jeans" is an inward-facing act, a project that works on the self, rather than the relatively outward-facing act of buying a well-known high fashion pair of jeans.

Conclusion

Anxiety has been recently re-evaluated as key to many fashion decisions made by individuals (Woodward 2007). There is anxiety over expected social responses to one's sartorial appearance and the anxiety about negotiating the balance between fitting in to a collective as well as standing out as an individual. Where vintage jeans in Japan are concerned, I argue that there is another anxiety that begs for resolution: "authenticity anxiety." Taylor-Atkins (2000) formulated the term to describe the dilemma he saw that Japanese jazz musicians had of having to be authentic through imitating the West: they were in the "awkward position of trying to authenticate themselves with reference to two very different standards—that of 'jazz' and that of 'Japanese culture'" (Taylor-Atkins 2000: 31). Not merely copying the *otehon* of vintage Levi's, but also "domesticating" (Tobin 1992) them through the strategies raised in this paper, has made it possible to express a Japanese identity through the American cultural product of jeans. This is not an anxiety that presents itself to all Japanese jeans wearers but it seems to affect the category of denim "maniacs," who are mostly men over thirty.

The "new vintage" super jeans of this paper support the Japanese version of authenticity that lies not in an original but in a copy achieved by using the same methods as those used to create the original (Hendry 2000; Moeran 1997). New models based on vintage Levi designs are not conceived of as inauthentic fakes but as faithful copies that, in being new, are even better than the real thing, the blemished original. The distressing processes achieve an even more perfect copy in that the jeans are rendered not as fashion but as worn work wear, in keeping with their original purpose. Non-distressed denim allows a different dimension of "real-ness" to be achieved through complicated wearing patterns that produce a pair of jeans that is unique to your body, authentic to your "self." In this way, in a saturated marketplace where consumption choices allow many "optional identities" (Lindholme 2008) personal authenticity is sought and achieved through wearing in a pair of these "super jeans."

This concern with rebranding (almost debranding) denim in terms of craft rather than fashion, and appealing to the wearer as holding the authentic owner relationship to the jeans over and above the company brand is typical of an increasing concern with authenticity in Japan. Japan, the "Empire of the Signs" (Barthes 1982) is often seen as an epitome of the post-modern society with all its free-floating symbolism: it follows that amongst this indiscriminate market where seemingly anything goes, there is an opposite movement that is obsessed in finding amongst this what is most "real."

A pair of blue jeans, like jazz (Taylor Atkins 2000), is a kind of "universal language"—so universal, in fact, as to be even "blindingly obvious" (Miller and Woodward 2007) and "culturally odourless" (Iwabuchi 2002), being easily domesticated globally despite their American origins. Whilst "blindingly obvious" in much of every day life, these "super jeans" are the result of taking even the most obvious aspects of jeans—the stitching, rivets and so on—and making them extraordinarily significant. The passionate investigation and pursuit of quality by many Japanese denim cognoscenti has resulted in an "exceptional authenticity" being successfully rendered for "Made in Japan" premium jeans. This authenticity, established fully in the 1990s in Japan, is now recognized globally, resulting in a slew of global high and quality fashion brands, ranging from the cult PRPS to Paul Smith, Dior and Savile Row tailors, using the "Made in Japan" quality as an authenticating strategy of their own.

Acknowledgment

I am grateful to the Hosei University International Fund for making this research possible.

Notes

1. Text on the website reads: "After our cotton is harvested in Africa, it is shipped to Japan and woven into denim cloth. PRPS denim is woven on vintage Levis shuttle looms that are wholly unlike the mass, projectile looms commonly used around the world today."

2. The names of some of the people and companies involved have been changed.

3. Pairs exist from as early as the late nineteenth century.

4. The suffix "xx" implies raw or "shrink-to-fit" denim.

5. Various vintages of "Levi's 501xx" was the answer most frequently given by the jeans makers interviewed in The Lightning Denim Book when asked, "What was the first pair of jeans you bought with the consideration of fashion?" They were also frequently cited as one of the makers' current favorite pairs, alongside those from their own denim brands.

6. Izuishi (1999: 244) also refers to this particular category of new vintage premium jeans as "refined jeans" using the word *ginjyou,* which means particularly refined or high quality with reference to *sake.*

7. This is often explained in terms of the Japanese having particularly sensitive skin but may be more rationally explained by the existence of only pre-worn *G-pan* before this point.

8. Kojima would unlikely to be known as a denim production center for anyone other than these cognoscenti or people in the industry.

9. In vintage Levi's this was run through with a red thread, and while red is used most commonly in repro-vintage denim, other colors are used too. Some companies make a "fake" selvedge on their cheaper jeans by stitching the frayed edges of projectile loom denim with red stitch, but it is too poor a likeness to be mistaken readily for the "real thing."

10. Some of the methods used on their jeans in general include washing at 90°C for an hour, washing with foreign objects from pumice stones to golf balls, using conditioners from various animal and plant products and so on.

11. Originally, hidden rivets were important for strengthening the work wear garments but now they are not used for such heavy-duty purposes and stitching techniques render them unnecessary.

References

Barthes, R. 1982. *Empire of Signs,* Trans. Richard Howard. New York: Hill & Wang.

Benjamin,Walter. 1992. *Illuminations.* London: Fontana.

Cox, R. (ed.). 2008. *The Culture of Copying in Japan.* Abingdon: Routledge.

Daniels, Inge. 2001. "The Fame of Miyajima: Spirituality, Commodification, and the Tourist Trade in Souvenirs in Japan," PhD Thesis, University College London.

Du Gay, P., Hall, S., Janes, L., Mackay, H. and Negus, K. 1997. *Doing Cultural Studies: The Story of the Sony Walkman.* Milton Keynes: Open University.

Gilmore, James H. and Pine, B. Joseph. 2007. *Authenticity: Contending with the New Consumer Sensibility.* Boston, MA: Harvard Business School Press.

Hendry, J. 2000. *The Orient Strikes Back*. Oxford: Berg.

Iwabuchi, K. 2002. *Recentering Globalization: Popular Culture and Japanese Transnationalism*. Durham, NC: Duke University Press.

Izuishi Shouzou. 1999. *Kanbon buru- ji-nzu*. Tokyo: Shinchousha.

Lightning (ed.). 2009a. *Studio D'artisan 30th Anniversary Book*. Tokyo: Ei Publishing.

Lightning (ed.). 2009b. *The Denim Book*. Tokyo: Ei Publishing.

Lindholme, C. 2008. *Culture and Authenticity*. Oxford: Blackwell.

Miller, D. and Woodward, S. 2007. "A Manifesto for a Study of Denim." *Social Anthropology* 2007(15): 335–51.

Moeran, Brian. 1997. *Folk Art Potters of Japan*. Richmond, Surrey: Curzon.

Peterson, R. A. 1997. *Creating Country Music: Fabricating Authenticity*. Chicago: University of Chicago Press.

Sugiyama, Shinsaku. 2009. *Nihon no buru-ji-nzu monogatari*. Okayama: Kibito.

Taussig, Michael. 2008. "Redeeming Indigo." *Theory, Culture and Society* 25(1): 1–15.

Taylor Atkins, E. 2000. "Can Japanese Sing the Blues?" in Craig, Timothy J. (ed.) *Japan Pop*. New York: Eastgate.

Tobin, Joseph J. (ed.). 1992. *Re-made in Japan*. New Haven, CT: Yale University Press.

Vann, Elizabeth F. 2006. "The Limits of Authenticity in Vietnamese Consumer Markets." *American Anthropologist* 108(2): 286–96.

Woodward, Sophie. 2007. *Why Women Wear What They Wear*. Oxford: Berg.

Yamane, Hidehiko. 2008. *Tateoti: Evisu the Photobook*. Tokyo: Ei Publishing.

Material Worlds: Denim on the Globalized Shop Floor

Abstract

This paper focuses on a material culture approach in order to explore multiple dimensions in the production of denim in an export-dominated assembly plant in Port Said, Egypt. Ethnographic data are analyzed to highlight the interplay between the surfaces and tools used in garment making and the skills and strategies deployed by factory workers, so elucidating some of the less immediately visible nuances in the turbulence of daily life on the production shop floor. Contrary to the common view that dismisses production tasks as repetitive and boring, these processes reveal the technical structures, skill hierarchies and uses of shop-floor language that give shade and variation to the skills attributed to different stages of "made-to-order" garment assembly work. These dynamics become more significant within the specific context of global and local competition for orders in which denim is established as the definitive fabric and brand through which reputations are made and sustained—for workers, for firms and for the city.

Keywords: denim, globalization, shopfloor, sociology, masculinity, gender, material culture

LEILA ZAKI CHAKRAVARTI

Leila Zaki Chakravarti trained as an anthropologist at the American University in Cairo. She worked as a shop-floor operative in an Egyptian garment assembly factory as fieldwork for her PhD studies (completed in 2009) at the School of Oriental and African Studies, London University. She is currently preparing her thesis for publication and exploring new research avenues into issues of gender in the "workplaces" of professional football.

Textile, Volume 9, Issue 1, pp. 62–75
DOI: 10.2752/175183511X12949158771473
Reprints available directly from the Publishers.
Photocopying permitted by licence only.
© 2011 Berg. Printed in the United Kingdom.

Material Worlds: Denim on the Globalized Shop Floor

Fabric as Framework

I worked as a shop-floor operative in a garment-assembly factory in the Export Processing Zone of Port Said (Egypt) for fourteen months (Chakravarti 2009). Most of this time the factory (which I shall call by the pseudonym Fashion Express—I also use pseudonyms in all references to the factory's personnel) was busy fulfilling orders for the assembly of denim garments. My visual memory is of a workspace piled high with stacks of partially completed denim items and, as I made my way home at the end of each working day, of the Zone's narrow alleys filled with puddles of indigo-stained water from the ceaseless washing of denim garments in neighboring factories. The economy of the Zone revolves around denim, the material that feeds the production lines of its garment factories. In this article I seek to shine a spotlight on the word "material" (as used in the previous sentence in the literal sense of "fabric") to reinterrogate my fieldwork data from the theoretical perspective of "material culture."

Daniel Miller has eloquently described the material culture approach as "a rather circuitous route to understanding people and relationships" (Miller 2010: 153). It is a line of intellectual analysis that focuses interest on "making things" and, at the same time, on "how things make people":

"Things, not, mind you, individual things, but the whole system of things, with their internal order, makes us the people we are. And they are exemplary in their humility, never really drawing attention to what we owe them" (Miller 2010: 53–4).

The material culture approach offers fresh criteria by which to view denim and the ideas associated with it during its transformation from raw material/fabric to finished "product." Once the objects and tools of labor, in the context of garment assembly, are laid open to scrutiny, it becomes possible to identify less visible linkages between various stages of the process, such as the specific instruments prominent in each stage of production; others that are improvised from more mundane objects to fill a void in the "making" process; the ideas and the structure of groups competing in completing an order; social hierarchies and how they translate into relationships of power at certain moments and not others. As a result a multitude of meanings surface to captivate us.

It is only recently that the literature on clothing and manufacturing has succeeded in accommodating qualitative intricacies of this type (Banerjee and Miller 2003; Halasa and Salam 2007; Küchler and Miller 2005; Snyder 2008). The fundamental contributions that earlier scholars made to the field (Elson and Pearson 1981; Enloe 1989; Joekes 1982) focused on the conditions under which labor was absorbed within outsourcing units, highlighting issues of exploitation, gender and patriarchy within current feminist debates. As a result an ingrained bias has taken hold, viewing tasks within a gendered, labor-intensive working environment as "boring" and "mechanical" (Visvanathan *et al.* 1997). Such generalizations are made easier when the objects used in garment assembling are invisible in these debates.

The view taken in this paper reverses the order of these arguments by bringing to center stage the tools and objects used in work on denim. This enables us to understand the ways multiple meanings can be generated through objectification; the relationships between materials and the individuals using them; and how the components of material culture become forms through which we sense complex possibilities of ourselves. The tools of labor and the different skills associated with a range of shop-floor objects provide a sensitive framework for analyzing how denim's social significance is constructed through the labor processes, especially if we see these objects as constructing the backdrop to the action through which denim is worked.

Management—Contract and Conception

The globalized garment industry is marked by cut-throat competition for orders in the face of "... capital flight, plant closure, transfer of operations and plant disinvestment" (Burawoy 1985: 150). Low-wage costs are no longer sufficient to attract international orders. Different countries, regions within a single country, cities within a single region and factories within a single city all strive to establish their competitive advantage through association with particular competencies, skill sets and capabilities (Collins 2003). Port Said is an Egyptian city at the Mediterranean mouth of the Suez Canal, whose export processing zone (EPZ) has, for some years now, sought to compete within the globalized garment assembly subcontracting chain by projecting an international reputation for specialist, cost-effective excellence in the cutting and assembling of garments fabricated from denim (as opposed to other fabrics). As is evident from even a cursory review of the websites of the twenty-four firms in the EPZ, the chosen image is one of "fashion houses" rather than mere garment factories, as firms have upgraded the facades of their premises to mimic the shopping malls and five-star hotels seen in Cairo or other cosmopolitan centers. The image is reinforced through graphics of super-cool youth in denim and sun shades, some in provocative poses, with samples of denim fashion items produced in the Zone listed alongside the commissioning international clients, including Gap, K-mart and Gloria (an Israeli brand). This narrative of denim as "international high-fashion" has evidently been identified by the proprietors and top management of the Zone's factories as their chosen solution to the problem of finding a distinctive niche in the competitive globalized garment industry, in effect of defining "the local within the global" (Miller 1995).

Fashion Express, in common with almost all firms in the Zone, maintains a strict separation between the conception and execution of all orders secured by top management. The former is the preserve of *edara* ("administration"—the firm's management), the latter the domain of *entag* (production). This feature is well documented in the literature, both in terms of theory (for example, Braverman 1974) and ethnography (for instance, Burawoy 1985). The most immediate manifestation of the segregation is in the physical construction and layout of the factory. As soon as one passes through the smoked-glass doors at the rear of top management's prestigious suite of offices, the space is separated into two levels: "upstairs" and "downstairs," identified respectively with the domains of *edara* and *entag*. The separation gives an impression of a "logical" order to the working environment of the firm, intended to demonstrate a level of integration and professionalism so that the production cycle of each denim order appears smooth and seamless.

Production studies is the first department in *edara* to cast a managerial "eye" on the incoming order. It sees its expertise as identifying the shop-floor *faniyyat* (techniques) that will be required in order to produce the new garment—referring to them collectively as *maharat* (a word for "skills", which elevates them above the level of manual laboring skills commonly classified as *san'a*). The required *faniyyat* are identified through a physical examination of *il-modil*, the specimen garment provided by the client, which is stretched out on a desk top. The new specimen is compared with the Department's "trophy rack" of examples of denim garment orders previously completed and commonly referred to as "Little and Large" (referring to the varying sizes of orders for different markets—from petite for the Far East, to XXL for the US).

The inspection process shows production studies' preference for *modilat sahla* (easy models) that reveal similarities with previous orders that have successfully emerged from the production floor, or that offer opportunities for developments in workforce skills. Denim, in particular, is considered to be a fabric with a "practical edge" in terms of upgrading skills within *entag*, either through repetition of existing skills, or incremental additions to skill-sets. The head of production studies elaborates on the principles that guide her choices:

> *Skills cannot be conjured up by clapping your hands! Workers build their portfolios of skills with orders that pass along the production pipe-line. Increasing orders of similar details achieves consistency in standards. When denim first made an appearance, it was then perceived as the* sha'bi *[common, working-class] style, the end of the fashion range. The general way of thinking is*

> *why not create a niche in the market? The* classic *is a style few factories in the Zone have the skills to undertake.*

Production studies also has a pragmatic preference for large-volume orders, in order to provide *entag* with scope for *yidhom takhud 'al-shughl* ("for their hand to grip the work")—with leeway to overcome initial teething troubles and produce items without faults in bulk.

From that point on the planning department becomes intimately involved. Its expertise rests in defining and monitoring the garment's trajectory along the shop-floor with a "scientific" mandate. It draws up a detailed plan that defines the separation of individual stages of *entag*, allocating the time each stage will be allowed to take. It also dispenses the necessary accessories to carefully guarantee a supply of monitored material to the shop floor. Every hour of the production day, teams of monitors descend the spiral staircase to the shop floor to count the hourly quotas produced by each assembly line. These multiple processes build a sustained profile of *entag's* progress in working according to plan.

The narratives that *edara* constitutes around denim can thus be seen to project an essentially unitary, static conception of "the workforce," which is articulated as a singular entity—one that, moreover, has changed only incrementally throughout the production of the previous "trophy" orders proudly displayed on the "Little and Large" rack.

Shop floor *maharat* (skills) are similarly spoken of in a static, undifferentiated sense—as generic capabilities possessed by "the workforce" as a unitary whole, rather than in terms of a range of different skills, developed (or lost) dynamically over time by a range of different units and individuals. This provides the basis for the "tried-and-tested" narrative of the factory's production that enhances the factory's "professional credibility" as it handles each denim order. The interesting questions to ask concern the extent to which these *edara* narratives around denim find resonance in *entag*. To explore this we need to descend from "upstairs" to the hubbub of the shop floor.

Cutting the Cloth—Ritual and Routine

The area of the shop floor, which *edara* overlooks, is occupied by *Qas*, the cutting department of *entag*, with the view "from upstairs" dominated by the white melamine surfaces of two long, narrow (20 meters by 2 meters) cutting tables. The production process begins when male workers known as *faraddin* (rollers) carry heavy rolls of denim from the materials warehouse and then work in pairs to run down the length of the tables, spreading the fabric. The unit supervisor then unrolls over the top layer a set of large paper patterns, which the design department has printed out from a computer disk provided by the client and ensures that these are stapled securely to the material. At each table *qas* workers (operating in pairs—one experienced cutter

with a junior and two pairs to a table) then wield industrial cutters, hanging from electric cables in the ceiling, to slice through the layers of denim according to the pattern marked. It requires strength, skill and concentration to guide the heavy, vibrating implements round the contours of each component, as if using a fretsaw to cut wood. Two supervisors inspect the cut components for defects, before they are moved to a much smaller (2 meters square) *tarqim* (marking) table in the corner, around which three female workers swing into action. Marking is a standing job, which requires a rapid wrist movement to flick through the layers of materials with one hand while with the other using a marking pistol to attach a sticker printed with a unique serial number to each item in the pile. The number identifies both the component and the layer of material from which it has been cut. This ensures that each assembled garment will be made up of components cut from the same layer of material to avoid small differences of color due to uneven dyeing of the denim. As Zizi, one of the unit supervisors says: "You can't put on a pair of jeans with the front not looking like the back. The differences in shades are quite specific to this type of cloth. It's its trademark—and you have to get it absolutely right!"

The material culture approach directs our attention to the "things" in use in the above processes, which in this case include not only the denim fabric being worked but also the implements the workers use and the surfaces on which they work. Views of the fabric appear to follow more-or-less logically from

its ease of handling at different stages of the process. *Faraddin* and cutters prefer lighter denims, since these are lighter to spread and easier to slice through. *Tarqim* workers, however, prefer heavier denim, which is easier to flick through: lighter denim is commonly spoken of as *omasha mi'afina* ("rotten fabric"), the choice of adjective infusing the fabric with human characteristics of "not being easy to get on with."

The names given by the workers to their tools and implements are also instructive. The "marking pistols" are simply *makanat tarqim* (marking instruments), while the "industrial cutters" are invariably referred to as *silah*, a noun that translates as "blade" or "weapon," conjuring up associations with the scimitars wielded by the knights of Arabic history and legend. This difference in verbal register can also be seen to be reflected in the ways in which these tools are deployed by their operators. *Tarqim* (marking) is a repetitious job where manual dexterity is required. The sound of *tarqim* is a loud, fast, rhythmic succession of bangs. Each *makana* has its own distinctive "bang," and is wielded at the distinctive pace of its operator. When three or four marking pistols are in use simultaneously the unit is consumed in its own sensory world. Overwhelmingly the impression is one of rapid *routine* repetition of a single task (albeit one more complex than might appear).

Cutting, conversely, is never a rushed job. After the unit supervisor has applied the paper stencil to the layers of spread fabric a mood of quiet expectation falls over the unit. The two most senior cutters approach the table, watched by the more junior members of their all-male team and the *farradin*. As they take up their *silah*, the senior cutters walk round the table staring at the stenciled pattern, deciding at which point to make the first incisions. Their concentration creates a moment's tension in the air until silent agreement is reached between them and they wield their heavy weapons, making the first cuts in the thick pile of fabric. The rapt attention of their audience is broken as, with a rush of adrenalin, a loud male cry of *Wil'a!* goes up (a meaningless word, used to celebrate a feat of prowess as when a football crowd celebrates a goal by the home team) providing the signal for the junior cutters to join in. The work demands not only mental concentration but also considerable strength and physical dexterity. Some cutters lean heavily on the table to force their implements through the layers of material. Others physically climb on top of the tables, straining in difficult postures as they guide the heavy *silah* round some particularly intricate tracings within the pattern, as both body and implement become supple instruments that embrace the cloth. The sound of several *silah* buzzing at once overpowers the human voices in the background, contributing to the sensation of a "masculine heat" and heightened emotion imbuing the whole performance. The overwhelming impression of cutting in action is one of *ritual*, in contrast to the *routine* of marking.

The ritual nature of the labor involved in cutting is confirmed by the manner in which *qas* alone is exempted from the detailed, time-bound quotas specified in *edara*'s "scientific" plan for the progression of the order through the various stages of *entag*. There appears to be a tacit recognition that such utilitarian metrics are not appropriate to this initial, ritual stage of the production process. Further evidence is provided by the way in which the senior cutters are referred to in the unit as *il-kommanduz* (the commandos), explicitly imbuing their workplace role with the same sort of martial significance with which the nickname *silah* invests the tools of their trade. Furthermore, cutters ignore management's requirement that a steel-mesh glove should be worn, preferring instead to display scars as "trophies," each with its own particular story behind it. These scars stand out as confirming their personal initiation, following a dangerous apprenticeship, into a select fraternity commanding both physical and social recognition within the workforce. There are resonances here with the Master Butchers summoned every Eid to the houses of the affluent to perform the ritual slaughter of a sacrificial sheep with a single blow of a specially sharpened knife, which is the prerogative of the initiated—leaving the subsequent dismemberment of the carcass as "clearing up" chores for the household cooks.

Focusing on the tools used at each stage enables us to identify significant differences: it is the interplay between the tool and the worker that gives each performance its distinctive characteristic of *ritual* or *routine*. Following Miller's approach, it also becomes evident that each performance is in turn shaped by the surface on which the performance is "staged," namely the differing physical constructions of the tables used in cutting and marking. The long, narrow, low construction of the cutting tables is as much a component of the emotionally heightened, masculinized ritual as is the *silah*, enabling the initiate *kommanduz* to walk around, lean on, and climb onto the piles of material. By contrast the small, square, waist-high shape of the *tarqim* table requires the workers to stand stationary around the edges, reaching onto the table in order to perform their allotted tasks. The result is that *tarqim* is constituted as the performance of a collective, fixed-position, predominantly feminine activity, demanding speedy (though by no means unskilled) repetition of a routine task—while cutting is constituted as the performance of an individual, mobile, masculine martial ritual. In each case worker, tool and table combine to different ends.

The shop floor is also active in developing a narrative around the skills involved in each of these differing labor functions (rolling, cutting and marking). *Faraddin* are seen, and see themselves, as at the bottom of the skills ladder—a peripheral position in which they have to "put in time" in order to be considered eligible candidates for a skilled apprenticeship. Their attempt to climb the skills ladder is exemplified by "Beckham," the nickname given to a twenty-year-old *farad* who approaches Khadija, a *tarqim* worker, for advice. Beckham spells out his frustration: "I want to be a *shakhsiyya* (a somebody).

I've been in this shit hole for two years!" Khadija occupies an undisputed matriarchal role among the all-female *tarqim* team and sums up his request in one phrase: "to be up-graded from a *bariza* (ten piastres) to a *rub' ginih* (twenty-five piastres)." Her strategy is to rely on drawing the attention of the supervisor by taking on Beckham as an extra pair of hands at the *tarqim* table. The physical transfer from one surface to the next would indirectly hint at a "natural progression" that would allow the supervisor to consider Beckham as a trainee. The female *tarqim* team acquiesces in this gender-crossing arrangement. Beckham struggles with the smaller pieces of cloth, groaning at his repeated clumsy mistakes and the array of wasted stickers around his work area. The girls watch his helplessness and remind him that "as a special favor" they have provided him with their best marking pistol, the one reserved as *makana lux*! Soon afterwards Beckham is given a chance with the *silah* when the cutting supervisor decides to try him out. By then two *kommanduz* have begun their own work, while the other *faradin* watch their colleague get his first try. Holding the heavy vibrating instrument, flushing and sweating profusely, Beckham begins to apply the *silah*. The *kommanduz* are in close physical proximity, and in low tones—as if whispering incantations—direct him in gliding the blade at a more steady pace. To dispel the fear and tension that grips the moment, Beckham's mates shout that "in the presence of a thousand and more spectators, Beckham gets it all the way through—unbeatable!"

Apart from the gender flexibility evident in pursuit of labor mobility, it can be seen from this account that the shop-floor has constructed a classification of skills that is different from the static *edara* narrative. Within the cutting department, a hierarchy of skills is constituted starting from the lowest level (*fard*) of unskilled "strength," moving dynamically upward to the next level (*tarqim*) of "manual dexterity" and then reaching the highest level (*qas*) of "strength plus manual dexterity." At each stage the definition and differentiation of skills is intertwined with the narratives of labor performance resulting from the physical surroundings as sets of living, shifting relations between people and objects.

Assembling Garments— Competition and Cohesion

The output of the cutting department feeds the two large assembly halls that form the heart of the entire operation, the lifeline of the factory. The process of assembling work is organized according to two principles: *tahdir* (preparation) and *tagmi'* (assembling), as well as in-line quality control inspection work. *Tahdir* is stationed towards one end of the hall, where a number of industrial machines are clustered together, demarcated not only spatially but also visually from the long, vertical rows of *tagmi'* machines in the main body of the hall. *Tahdir* is engaged in stitching and piecing together small components such as pockets and loops that are affixed to the garment during the *tagmi'* process. Each machine in the *tagmi'* stage is engaged in a single *marhala* (sewing task), after which the garment is passed to the next machine. Depending on the design, a garment can easily pass through thirty separate stages of being unfolded, worked and folded again before *tagmi'* is completed. Monitors at in-line quality control (QC) stations closely scrutinize and monitor each partially assembled garment at regular stages. Each vertical row of six machinists faces a QC and finished garments pass through at least six in-line QC checks until they pile up in large metal containers to be wheeled out for final quality control, laundry/ironing and packaging.

The welter of sensory perceptions that give the spatial landscape of assembly its manufacturing definition can be overwhelming—the intensity of the ceaseless din of machinery, the shouted voices, the ringing of mobile phones, the distinctive color schemes of the denim orders, the oppressive heat and the turbulence of large numbers of human bodies. Workers are stationary behind their sewing machines or quality-control stands while supervisors (predominantly female) demonstrate their rank and fulfill their defined role of *yishaghal il-khat* ("working the assembling line") through incessant motion within the sea of machinery and bodies and self-consciously exaggerated physical "performance" described in shop-floor slang as *yi wir* ("going round in circles"). They push partially completed garments from one station to the next as they count items and note down on sheets of paper the production volumes churned out by each section along the line. Every so often they pause and gaze at the workers around them, then pounce swiftly to correct some perceived individual inadequacy or error. They shout dramatically at workers, waving their arms in dramatic gestures in order to keep production flowing and on target.

The exact arrangement of the industrial machinery and the deployment of individual workers along the assembly lines are readjusted each time a fresh denim order is begun. This rearrangement is initiated by the production manager, who acts as the interface between *edara* and *entag*, and verbally informs the shop-floor supervisors of *edara*'s high-level plan for the spatial positioning of sewing machines and workforce, which changes according to their assessment of the specific requirements of each order. For instance, the two assembling halls may be compelled to work sequentially on the same order: one committed to *tahdir*, the second to *tagmi'*. In another arrangement the two halls can be required to work quite independently from one another, each given a separate order. In a still more common arrangement, a large denim order may be divided unequally between the two assembling halls for each to assemble from scratch. In each case, however, the *amr tashghil* (scheme of work) designed by *edara* prescribes the *intagiyya* (quota of garments) to be produced each hour of the working day.

This high-level scheme is translated into operational specifics by the shop-floor supervisors who discuss and agree a detailed plan for what is known as *tandif il-khat* ("cleansing the assembling lines"). This procedure involves pooling their detailed knowledge and experience of the shop floor to work out how and where to move various items of machinery and draw up a new division of tasks among squads of workers. This elaborate process relies on what is described as *il-'ain* ("the eye"), the visual expertise of senior workers who together are able, by consensus, accurately to assess details related to the fine stitches and other requirements of different *tahdir* and *tagmi'* components. On the face of things, the supervisors' agreed plan for *tandif il-khat* appears solely geared to implementing—in practical, on-the-ground shop-floor detail—the high-level *amr tashghil* conveyed "from upstairs" by the production manager. By focusing on the interplay between the "things" (in this case the fabric being worked, and the machinery and tools used to work it) and the people (in this case the workers and their supervisors) involved, other narratives can also be identified which underpin—or contest—the surface appearances: one parallels the cutting department's differentiation of a hierarchy of workforce skills, and the other is around competition for power and status on the shop floor.

When rotating their workforce squads for each new work order, supervisors focus closely on the skills and potential of each individual worker in their particular unit. They see their ability to form "skill configurations" as giving them control over the deployment, and the development, of their workers' skills levels. New recruits

to the assembly halls often begin their employment as ancillary workers, a position where they can demonstrate their potential for upgrading. As Horriya, the senior-most Assembly Hall Supervisor (and universally respected as, in effect, Foreman for the entire factory) remarks:

> I started that way myself, twenty years ago—it's the way we grew to love the work ... Ancillary workers make the best machinists, even as their current post appears of minor importance, marking pieces of cloth with pencil and chalk. As they sit next to the machinists they spend hours watching, their bodies and minds, absorbing the system over many days, weeks, months. They watch as garments pass from one machinist to the next, the frenzy and excitement of the "mood" and pick up invaluable tips on how to resolve small details in garment work. By the time they are seated behind the sewing machine, they are almost there. It's also the case that they prefer to pick up the skills that way. I strongly believe that ruh il-khat ["the soul of the assembly line"] is the true master of the skills and values associated with our environment: loyalty, precision, competitiveness, team work— and a burning desire not to be defeated!

When redeploying staff for each new denim order, supervisors focus on identifying those who possess *qodra* (the potential) to move up the ladder of skills. An ancillary worker can be moved to a sewing machine with a simple task and

then to more complex machinery and tasks. Over the course of several denim orders of different complexity machinists can attain the most highly prized position of all, that of a multi-skilled worker known on the shop-floor as a *joker*. *Jokers* are prized for their versatility in countering *ad hoc* shortages of labor, as they can be moved around the assembly line with ease. These positions are highly prestigious when compared to the less-skilled machinist positions known as *marhala sabta* (fixed position). There is also the unspoken, tacit advantage that *jokers* do not require direct supervision from supervisors. The freedom to organize their workload gives them immense power within their teams. They act as pace makers to push their teams at critical points in the working day. So while meeting the high-level plans of *edara*, the re-organization of assembly's machinery and workers for each new denim order can thus be seen as also constituting a sub-narrative around the definition of a hierarchy of shop-floor skills, and the dynamic progression (or regression) of individual workers within it.

Horreya's paean to the *ruh il-khat* included specific references to the competitive features of shop-floor production. At one level this can be understood as expressing *entag*'s resistance to a perceived hidden agenda underlying the drawing up by *edara* of each new order's *amr tashghil*, one that seeks to "keep the shop-floor on its toes" by fomenting rivalry between different units and individuals. Requiring the two assembly halls to work on the same order, either sequentially or in parallel, is seen as establishing different degrees of competition between them—whilst requiring each to work exclusively on a different order is interpreted as management providing a period of respite so that shop-floor competition does not damage the overall unity of the firm.

If, however, we focus on the interplay between the people and "things" in the assembly halls, a more subtle degree of shop-floor competition becomes apparent. A unit will suddenly find that its supply of brand tags has "gone missing," or that the bobbins of thread for its machines have been "stolen" by another unit. Or a unit may find that the most reliable of its sewing machines have mysteriously been removed elsewhere within the factory, with workers from another unit swarming over them claiming possession—a strategy common enough for the shop-floor to have developed its own slang to describe this form of *sirqa fi 'izz il-nahar* ("theft in broad daylight"). Sometimes a supervisor will be dismayed to find that, just as the *edara* monitors come down for their end-of-day count and are in a hurry to get home, workers from a rival unit have surreptitiously switched the handwritten signs identifying her own unit's piles of *intagiyya* (production) as either *fahs* (finished) or *islah* (for repair). Incidents also occur in which workers themselves becomes pawns in such inter-unit rivalry, as when a senior supervisor pulls rank and assigns workers who are known to be weak at the job to a more junior supervisor—a tactic also recognized by its own shop-floor label as *biwaka' il-khat*

("bringing down the assembly line"). The receiving supervisor's defensive tactics can include giving the inferior workers imposed on her the most defective scissors at her disposal so that she in turn can point the finger at the poor skills development that the workers have received under their previous unit's supervisor.

Yet picking up Miller's insight that "the more we fail to notice things, the more powerful and determinant of us they turn out to be" (Miller: 2010: 54) leads us to focus on the unspoken substrate for the above maneuvers, namely the fabric being worked on by the people, machines and implements which are the subjects of such intense contention—denim itself. Assembly workers are aware that denim is the chosen emblem of the entire Zone's narrative of its distinctive international competitiveness. They also see for themselves, on a daily basis, the way in which denim provides the narrative for intra-Zone competition between different firms—for example during lunch breaks, when workers from adjacent factories mingle in the narrow alleyways and exchange competitive banter about the relative status and merits of the denim brands their respective factories are working on. In these ways denim comes to be constituted as the "stuff" of competition—and it can thus be seen as hardly surprising that it should also be the catalyst for competition within the walls of a single factory.

Although the ceaseless shop-floor rivalry between different supervisors and their units can be intense, its overall effect is cohesive rather than divisive. At one level these manifestations of rivalry are framed as "playing the game" in a contest in which they are all mutually joined—indeed, being a player is an essential part of what "being an assembly worker" is. If the dynamic is one of mutual rivalry, there is just as much significance attached to the "mutuality" of it all as there is to the "rivalry." At a second level, however, there exists a subtle understanding that the common objective is to "cock a snook" at *edara* by demonstrating that the fine precision of their scientifically designed schemes are unrealistic when translated to the brutal realities of the "real world." If the *amr tashghil* and its hourly quotas are to be shown to be other worldly then production cannot be allowed to move according to plan—and it is the stops and starts, peaks and troughs of real-life *entcg* that ensure that this happens. A breakdown in one unit soon leads to a "pile up" as the output of the preceding units on the line continues to flow into it, requiring the drama of loud recrimination and remedial action. The analogy with the noisy and congested traffic on the streets of Egypt's major cities is deliberately invoked in the choice of shop-floor slang by which *edara*'s scientific *amr tashghil* is referred to as *il-manifesto*, a word commonly used in the outside world to refer to the published timetable for a bus route—which never moves according to plan. The usage draws on Egypt's long-standing tradition of political humor, commenting on the gap between what parties proclaim they can promise and what is actually delivered.

A third level of cohesiveness becomes apparent from the way in which rivalry and competition is never allowed to develop to the point that the delivery of an order is placed at risk. However many stops and starts there may have been along the way, *entag* pulls together to ensure that the contracted volumes are delivered by the stipulated deadlines. As the supply of raw denim runs out in cutting, workers are transferred to help out units such as packaging to ensure that the job is completed on time. This constitutes a final reaffirmation of everyone's common membership of the firm, making real management's favorite slogan of *masna' wahid, id wahda* ("one factory, one hand").

Conclusion

In this article I have adopted a material culture approach to reinterrogate my fieldwork data and so have highlighted the multiplicity of narratives that are constituted when the top management, middle management and workforce of a factory assembling denim garments for the globalized market activate the dynamics between "how things are made by people" and "how people are made by things." To top management, denim is the chosen vehicle for defining the factory's and the Zone's distinctive international advantage within the cut-throat competition that characterizes the supply chains of the globalized garment industry. To middle management denim is the template against which to assess the factory's skills base, albeit within an essentially static view of the production process. But the shop-floor's treatment of denim

reveals that the garment assembly process involves the constant recreation and re-enactment of a welter of differing narratives around the materials, tools and skills of labor. These different perspectives, narratives and "orders of things" remain the touch points that the operation returns to reaffirm both the individual and collective identity of the workplace.

References

Banerjee, Mukulika and Miller, Daniel. 2003. *The Sari*. Oxford: Berg.

Braverman, Harry. 1974. *Labor and Monopoly Capital: The Degradation of Work in the Twentieth Century*. New York: Monthly Review Press.

Burawoy, Michael. 1985. *The Politics of Production*. London: Verso.

Chakravarti, Leila Zaki. 2009. "Made in Egypt. Gender, Class and Religion on the Globalized Shop-Floor." PhD thesis, SOAS, University of London.

Collins, Jane. 2003. *Threads. Gender, Labor and Power in the Global Apparel Industry*. Chicago: University of Chicago Press.

Elson, Diane and Pearson, Ruth. 1981. "The Subordination of Women and the Internalization of Factory Production." In Kate Young, Carol Wolkowitz and Roslyn McCullagh (eds) *Of Marriage and the Market: Women's Subordination in International Perspective*, pp. 144–66. London: CSE Books.

Enloe, Cynthia. 1989. *Bananas, Beaches and Bases: Making Feminist Sense of International*

Politics. Berkeley: University of California Press.

Halasa, Malu and Salam, Rana. 2007. *The Secret Life of Syrian Lingerie*. Scalo: Prince Claus Fund.

Joekes, Susan. 1982. *Female-headed Industrialization: Women's Jobs in Third World Export Manufacturing*. IDS Research Report no 15. Brighton, Sussex: Institute of Development Studies.

Küchler, Susanne and Miller, Daniel (eds). 2005. *Clothing as Material Culture*. Oxford: Berg.

Miller, Daniel (ed.). 1995. *Worlds Apart: Modernity through the Prism of the Local*. London: Routledge.

Miller, Daniel. 2010. *Stuff*. Cambridge: Polity.

Snyder, Louise Rachel. 2008. *Fugitive Denim. A Moving Story of People and Pants in the Borderless World of Global Trade*. New York, London: W. W. Norton & Company.

Visvanathan, N., Duggan, L., Nisonoff, L. and Wiegersma, N. (eds). 1997. *The Women, Gender and Development Reader*. London: Zed Books.

"Cowboy Cloth" and Kinship: The Closeness of Denim Consumption in a South-West Chinese City[1]

Abstract

This article examines the effect of the fabric denim in objectifying kinship in the city of Kunming, China. It is argued that denim has been particularly efficacious due to its ability to insert itself into traditional Chinese kinship notions of nurturance. Parents were seen to gift denim to their children with the object of instigating a change in the lives of the younger generation, coupled with the knowledge that a change in material circumstances would be necessary to achieve such transformation. At the same time, the younger generation's denim also provoked a "kinship gulf" between children and their parents, which parents appeared keen to close by purchasing and wearing denim of their own (although not without a degree of ambivalence, reflected by the presence of inactive jeans in parents' wardrobes). In this remarkable situation denim was seen, firstly, as the tool for creating generational disjuncture through traditional means and subsequently as the prospective solution to overcome this disjuncture. It is argued here that denim moves us to consider the study of kinship as the study of "closeness," a term that affords the consideration of objects in the milieu of intimate social relationships.

Keywords: China, closeness, comfort, denim, family, kinship, nurturance

TOM McDONALD

Tom McDonald is a research student in the Department of Anthropology at University College London. He also occupies a Visiting Research Scholar position at the Nationalities Research Institute in Yunnan University, China. Tom is currently undertaking fieldwork on denim consumption in small-town south-west China.

Textile, Volume 9, Issue 1, pp. 76–89
DOI: 10.2752/175183511X12949158771518
Reprints available directly from the Publishers.
Photocopying permitted by licence only.

"Cowboy Cloth" and Kinship: The Closeness of Denim Consumption in a South-West Chinese City[1]

For office administrator Zhang Guangli, talk of jeans invokes vivid recollections of an event from his childhood. When he was in the third year of primary school in Kunming, towards the autumn of 1983, political factions in the Chinese Communist Party launched the "anti-Spiritual Pollution" campaign. The campaign targeted what was perceived as an increase in damaging Western ideals, which were seen as having entered the country following the declaration of the "open door" policy five years earlier. Propaganda initially attacked pornography, trends in art and literary and theoretical thinking; however, its scope was soon extended to bring a far wider range of social phenomena under criticism (Gold 1984: 947). At the height of the campaign, Guangli recalled, his school decreed that jeans, by that time popular attire for himself and his classmates, were "spiritually polluting." Suddenly, not a student was to be seen wearing denim, either at school or in the public sphere. Guangli recalled his mother taking pains to ensure that he did not wear jeans during this period because of the risk of bringing himself or the family into disrepute. The campaign itself was quietly wound down in early 1984 but for a brief moment, at least, jeans became the center of attention. Even though only young people were wearing denim at the time, their regulation in this period was a concern for the entire family.

This article demonstrates that although denim (*niúzǎibù*; literally "cowboy cloth")[2] may now no longer be seen as "spiritually polluting," its appropriation continues to provide a means by which family relations are materialized. It concerns itself with the ramifications of denim consumption in the formation of kinship in contemporary Kunming, a south-western Chinese city in the throes of rapid deveopment.[3] Social changes have created an explosion in opportunities for consumption of mass-produced products, an increase in transactions, and the production of consumptive desires, known as the "consumer revolution" in China (Davis 2000: 7).

It is in this context that denim has appeared and proliferated. The researcher's own (very rough) headcount on a commercial street in the center of the city revealed forty-four out of 100 passers-by were wearing denim. In Kunming's residential suburbs this figure decreased to twenty-three out of 100. Denim was selected because, as Miller and Woodward (2007: 337) argue, it is the worldwide ubiquity of jeans, combined with the lack of attention research affords them, which means that they can actually have a *greater* possibility of revealing insights into fashion, clothing and the act of dressing than perhaps any other item.[4]

Anthropological approaches to Chinese society have long been steeped in the social anthropological tradition, emphasizing the study of kinship as "the recognition of a relationship between persons based on descent or marriage" (Stone, 1997: 5). Anthropologists such as Morgan (1871: 415), Lévi-Strauss (1969: 328) and Freedman (1965) were largely responsible for forming the classic model of the Chinese kinship system: consanguineal in nature, agnatic, emphasizing patrilineality, reinforced through a complex array of vocatives and the corporate institution of the family.[5]

Following the founding of the People's Republic of China, family relations underwent significant upheaval. Such changes may be attributed to a number of factors, including allocation of childcare through communes and later compulsory education (Kipnis 2008), the right to divorce (Diamant 2000: 128) and, perhaps most significantly, the one-child-one-family policy (Fong 2004). China's youth has benefited from increasing economic and political power in the family, which has, it is claimed, effectively disrupted the traditional agnatic system and the emphasis on filial piety (for accounts see Yan 2003: 89, 2004: 148, 2005: 637). Various narratives have noted that this has accompanied what Simmel

(1978: 448) terms the increase in material culture.

This paper takes the radical item of denim, and grounds it in the traditional anthropological analytic framework of Chinese kinship studies. It is argued that denim has been particularly efficacious due to its ability to insert itself into the traditional Chinese notion of nurturance (*yăng*), which Stafford (1995: 80, 2000) describes as the wide array of symbolic and substantive transfers between parent and child that places an obligation on offspring to reciprocate the care received in youth when they reach adulthood. The obligation to return *yăng* continues even after parents die, with the burning of paper clothing (and paper money) to comfort deceased ancestors (Doolittle, 1866: 61; Gates, 1987). Zhao and Belk (2003) also found that modern consumer goods are being incorporated into these practices. They observed the inclusion of paper cell phones, computers, PDAs, televisions, refrigerators, stereos and automobiles being burnt in ancestral offerings.

These studies highlight a discourse that privileges clothing as an essential form of nurturance, on par with food, and fundamental for the creation of kinship relations. Stafford (1995: 100) illustrates this through a mother's concern over judgments of her appearance that might be made by others on visiting her son. The son's ability to *yăng* his mother, Stafford claimed, was expressed in the clothes she wore, "while their ability to care for (*yăng*) each other was reflected in the food they, as a family, could serve to someone from the outside."

In this context it therefore seems reasonable to postulate that denim allowed parents to maintain traditional parent-child nurturing roles by clothing their children while simultaneously fulfilling the motive of instigating a transformation in the lives of their descendants, coupled with the knowledge that a change in material circumstances would be necessary to achieve such transformation.

However, the denim given to the younger generation also provoked a "kinship gulf" between children and their parents that parents have more recently appeared keen to close by purchasing and wearing denim of their own (though not without a degree of ambivalence, reflected by, for example, inactive jeans present in parents' wardrobes). Denim in Kunming was thus seen firstly as the tool creating generational disjuncture through traditional means and subsequently as the prospective solution to remove this disjuncture.

Finally, this article will demonstrate that the study of denim not only engenders contemplation of the textile in terms of objectifying kinship but also prompts a reconsideration of what the study of kinship should be. It is herein argued that denim points us to consider the study of kinship as the study of "closeness," a term that affords the consideration of objects in the milieu of intimate relationships.

Denim and the Dongs

The case of the Dong family will now be examined as it exemplifies the distribution of denim that seems commonplace among families. The researcher's main contact with the Dong family came through twenty-two year-old Dong Baiyi. Dong Baiyi lives at home with her older brother and parents and, as such, they live in a nuclear kinship unit. The Dong family is atypical of modern Chinese kinship structure in that they have two children due to an exemption in the family planning laws allowing couples in which one of the parents is of a state-recognized ethnic minority (Dong Baiyi's mother, Li Jingmei, is of Dai ethnicity) to have multiple births (Sautman 1998: 89–90).

The family is economically comfortable. Dong Baiyi works as a receptionist in a two-star hotel, earning around 2000 RMB per month. Her brother, Dong Yishan, sells insurance, which can earn several thousand RMB per month dependent on commission. Baiyi's father, Dong Guoping, is a traditional Chinese medicine (TCM) doctor and her mother is a nurse.

Dong Baiyi claims only she and her brother wear denim regularly while her parents wear it very rarely. Baiyi herself had six pairs of jeans and her brother had four pairs. The presence of denim in the family, however, is not a new phenomenon—it dates back to 1990, when Baiyi was only four years old. At that time she received a denim dress from her mother's sister who, Baiyi informed the researcher, was then making a living importing large amounts of foreign clothing for sale.

The purchase of Baiyi's first pair of jeans occurred six years later, at her request, when ten-year-old Baiyi was in the final year of primary school. Baiyi was able to vividly recall the event:

Yes, because I thought in school, very many people were wearing [jeans]. I thought they were very beautiful. So I made my Dad take me. It [jeans] had just become popular ...

At that time I felt ... at that time I bought them ... that cloth was very, very soft. I felt, the color was very light. Light blue. Light blue. At that time. Afterwards, below it had Mickey mouse design. I felt, at that time I felt it was very fashionable, the important thing was I felt it was very popular, ah, to have flared-trousers, it didn't feel bad at all. Also, I recall at that time I unexpectedly had a little bit of an interest in denim. Because I felt when you wear them it was very comfortable, not the same as other trousers, where you wear them for a few days, they're dirty ... with denim, you don't have to wash it so clean.

Baiyi's third denim item, another pair of jeans, was gifted from her father's elder brother, who gave her a set of tight jeans, which she claims to have disliked. Her fourth denim item, given to her shortly afterwards, was a pair of dungaree jeans:

Baiyi: *And that time, ah ... too cute! I felt wearing dungaree jeans, I felt relatively cute. After, I just really liked to wear [them], because braced jeans are very convenient, just a T-shirt and some braced trousers. I felt very good.*

Interviewer: *Your friends, at that time, also wore them?*

Baiyi: *Yes. I think from the sixth year of primary school,* *starting that time, it started to become fashionable. Just, a lot of little girls who love to make themselves up and wear beautiful clothes started to wear them, just started to wear jeans.*

Baiyi's testimony reveals important trends for her induction into denim. All four of the first denim items she received were gifted to her, with at least three of those coming from close relations on both the maternal and paternal sides of her family. Baiyi herself took an active role in instigating the purchase of one pair.

Today Baiyi's situation has changed. She now has a university degree, a job and considerable autonomy over her clothes, food and lifestyle. She continues to live at home but the flow of resources has started to reverse itself, perhaps most significantly by the surrender of a third of her monthly income (around 600 RMB) to her parents. This reverse reveals, in some sense, Baiyi's filial obligation to her parents to return the nurturance she has been given. However, in this period denim has continued to remain an important feature in Baiyi's wardrobe, even if the way she has thought about them has changed:

Now I like jeans because they are convenient (fāngbiàn), *you can match them with anything. Match them with T-shirts, match them with shirts. And ... the main point is you can match them with anything. Also, they won't be vulgar* (yōngsú).

Baiyi's denim collection has expanded to six pairs of jeans (only three of which she regularly wears) a pair of denim dungarees and three denim dresses. Baiyi's jeans are not particularly tight and many have floral designs.

The importance of floral forms in Baiyi's life quickly became apparent. Virtually every time Baiyi met the researcher she was wearing at least one item of clothes featuring some kind of floral pattern. This ranged from a pink hooded top with large flowers on it to small flowers on the inner lining of her *Converse*-style shoes, the tongue of which was folded over to reveal the floral-patterned fabric. But flowers were not merely worn by Baiyi, they seemed to permeate her entire life. This was made apparent when Baiyi invited the researcher on a park trip to "look at the flowers" (kànhuā). Baiyi was able to identify a large array of flora, their blossoming times and sometimes their medicinal use. On at least three separate days she pointed out or drew the researcher's attention to flowers.

Baiyi is aware that her clothing differs markedly from that of her parents. Her father owns only a single pair of jeans (which he rarely wears); her mother owns three; in comparison to four owned by her brother and six by herself. Baiyi reported that none of her grandparents (both paternal and maternal) ever owned or wore jeans. She describes their style as "plain" (pǔsù), although she said that she did not mind the clothes that they wore. Baiyi's mother also wore a long, very flowery skirt on the occasion she met the researcher. In fact, the amount of casual skirts in her mother's wardrobe exceeded

Baiyi's own. Baiyi related her mother's preference for skirts to her Dai ethnicity. Regardless of the garment, though, the wearing of flowers, either embroidered or print, seemed to be something that both she and her mother could indulge in, linking the maternal side and emphasizing femininity.

Baiyi has been wearing denim for over four-fifths of her life and jeans for over half. Baiyi likes jeans because they are "comfortable" and "convenient"—two words she used on countless occasions to describe jeans. Denim has grown with her, and her preferences in what constitutes suitable denim have changed. Most of her jeans remain straight-legged or flared, which she maintains is appropriate if your body is "just ok." Flowers emphasize her femininity but also draw attention to her body. The cut of Baiyi's denim enables her to be a grown woman while still being a filial daughter. The history of her receiving the denim from her family represents a tacit approval of her choice by her parents, which has enabled her to expand the forms of denim she wears. The multiple forms of denim that Baiyi owns suggest that the fabric was instrumental in allowing this transformation of identity to occur.

The Selfless Jean? Denim and Nurturance

The young age at which Dong Baiyi received her first pair of denim jeans reflects the oft-encountered role that parents had in encouraging their offspring to adopt denim. In all four of the families included in this fieldwork, the youngest generation owned, on average, double the amount of denim items owned by their parents.

The role parents played in encouraging their children to wear denim was reflected in a number of ways. First, in shopping trips, the near-universal accompaniment of under-18 year olds by parents or grandparents was observed. Parents not only sanctioned the purchase but frequently handed over the money themselves.

Many young adults described starting university as a breakpoint, in terms of shopping unaccompanied, citing the freedom to shop on their own or with friends. However, most still received some sort of allowance from their parents to spend on clothing. Twenty-one year-old female student Luo Huidai summarized the situation:

> Before I had started university, I lived with my mother, she would take me to stroll the streets (guàngjiē), and provide ideas, but after starting university Mum was not by my side. Every month we receive living expenses, right? ... [Now] when we stroll the streets ... I go with classmates, there are a few people whose perspective (yǎnguāng) will be about the same as [me]. I will get these people to accompany me to buy ... I will get at least another person to come with me. Because a friends' eyes are like a mirror.

The most extreme example of familial shopping strategies observed was that of Yang Changying. Changying was accompanied on the shopping trip by her mother's sibling's daughter (younger than Changying) (*biǎomèi*). Changying found a top and a pair of high heels she particularly liked and resolved to purchase them. However, the seller only gave a 5 RMB discount on her original asking price of 180 RMB. Changying became particularly irate at the fact that the seller would not give her a larger discount. She marched out of the stall, boarded a taxi, and went across town to a large seven-floor market, where her mother's other sibling's daughter (older than Changying) (*biǎojiě*), who she simply addressed as "older sister" (*jiě*), had a small stall. "Older sister" then took the lead in sourcing the rest of Changying's costume with items from her own stall at cost price and, using her hard-nosed bargaining skills, some pieces from nearby stalls at heavily discounted prices. Under her "older sister's" supervision she managed to get a new t-shirt, tights, some black shorts and a pair of high-heeled shoes for 100 RMB.

Changying's case, though not directly about denim (even though she was wearing jeans at the time), illustrates the enduring importance of Chinese kinship relations in the procurement of clothing, even in urban environments. When formal methods of obtaining clothing with strangers through economic methods failed, Changying reverted to an extended family network to obtain clothing at an affordable price.

The first finding of this paper is that parents in Kunming have, since the start of China's opening and reform period in the early 1980s, elected to clothe their offspring in denim while, in most instances, not choosing to follow the trend themselves. They have achieved this through buying and gifting clothes to young children and through the tacit approval gained through the act of accompanying older children on shopping trips, where they are also often frequently called upon to fund the purchase. Denim, however, seems to have a separate story to tell in this context—that is, of parents' own unease about the disjuncture that has been created, and their subsequent attempts to close it.

Parental Attempts to Close the Kinship Gulf

In the case of the Dong family, both of the parents owned denim items but the researcher never observed either of the parents wearing them. This observation was further substantiated by the daughter, Dong Baiyi, who testified that her parents rarely wore the denim they owned. This phenomenon was by no means confined to the Dong family. In all the families surveyed, parents reported that they owned denim but through regular encounters in the course of their day-to-day lives it became plainly obvious that they very rarely wore their jeans. None of the families reported grandparents as ever having owned or worn jeans.

Gao Suyin, 45, who worked at a vegetable stall was a notable exception to this. Gao Suyin was noted to alternate two pairs of trousers on the days she worked at the stall. Some days she wore a pair of smart cotton patterned grey/ black trousers, on other days she wore a rather ill-fitting pair of jeans. Unusually for a woman of her age, the jeans were relatively tight on

her body, the waist of which was pulled up to her navel. They had two off-center seams on the outside and the bottom three inches were folded up around her shin. She had bought the jeans for her daughter who had refused to wear them. Chinese markets generally do not issue refunds for unwanted goods so she ended up wearing them herself.

Several parents remarked on what they perceived to be the inconvenience of jeans in comparison to 'casual trousers' (*xiūxiánkù*). For example, Chen Juan and her husband are both in their forties, and run a small boiled dumpling restaurant in the North-west of the city. She explained that though she does own some jeans, she does not wear them. She says that older people should wear looser, more relaxed clothes, rather than "tight, tight, stretched, stretched" (*jǐnjǐnběngběng*) ones. Juan put her statement into practice the following day when she was observed wearing a huge, grey sleeveless, loose one-piece smock-like outfit with strips of dark-gray acrylic fur along the edges.

That is not to say that denim is completely absent from the Chen family. On one occasion, Chen Juan's brother-in-law who also worked at the restaurant, perched at the end of the restaurant and lit up a cigarette. His trousers appeared to be denim-like except they were not "standard" denim: they consisted of pale blue, very thin cotton. On the back pocket were ornate embroidered flowers in dark blue thread. His keys and a pair of nail clippers hung from his belt. Jutting out from underneath his jeans were a pair of shiny white, alligator-skin style loafers,

with a small golden-colored flash on them. As he made to leave, he donned a pair of tinted glasses, mounted his blue electric scooter, cigarette hanging from mouth, and rode away. The two sisters looked at each other, and were overheard disparagingly saying: "His clothes, they're so bad looking" (*tā de yīfu tài nánkàn*). Hong Jianhua's sartorial digression provoked disapproval precisely because his choice of items was not suitable for a man of his age and position.

In fact, the ownership of such trousers, typically made of soft blue cotton fabric was not at all uncommon among middle-aged parents. They were made to look slightly distressed, like jeans, although they felt more like the cotton "casual trousers" preferred by parents. When Dong Baiyi told the researcher that her father had just such a pair of "jeans," she also disparagingly remarked, "They're not proper jeans, though."

Color was another important differentiating factor between parents and their children's adoption of the fabric. Denim was available in a range of colors in Kunming; however, the most popular remained blue. It was more common for the lowest generation to experiment with wearing different colors, while parents preferred blue jeans, which one informant described as being more "traditional" (*chuántǒng*).

Children and young people wore a far wider range of denim styles than did adults. Parents seemed to be restricted in style mostly to jeans whereas young people were also seen wearing dungarees and skirts. Children were perhaps the only group to also wear full denim suits (jackets and jeans) in addition to the styles. In the research period, a pair of heavily distressed, torn jeans, which are known in China by the nickname "beggars' trousers" (*qǐgàikù*) were spotted only once, worn by a twenty-something female.

In conclusion, having effectively "weaned" their children onto a variety of denim forms, most parents opted not to actively follow the path they had sent their own offspring down. Wang Baiyi recounted the pairs of jeans that hung, unused, in her parents' wardrobes. Chen Juan had a pair of unused jeans that she disliked for their lack of comfort and overall tightness. The jeans Guo Suyin purchased for her daughter had been rejected and by default fell to her to wear, which she did so in the workplace, despite them being somewhat ill fitting. Parents would happily say that denim looked good on their own offspring but that it was not suitable for themselves. One possible explanation for this phenomena may be that these parents are likely to have witnessed, or been aware of, the criticism leveled at denim as "spiritually polluting" by the state apparatus in the 1980s (see Wang 1986; Webb 1986; He 1996 for accounts) and, more broadly, the severe repercussions of sartorial indiscretions during the cultural revolution when wrongdoers were forced to remove offending garments in front of crowds during Red Army struggle sessions (Nien 1987: 85; in Steele and Major 1999: 59). It is possible that such memories generate the ambivalence felt by parents towards wearing denim themselves.

If parents really experience such feelings of anxiety because of their experience of the previously hazardous nature of denim, what could account for their decision to purchase the jeans in the first place and then subsequently not wear them? Parents did not provide any testimony as to the logicality of their purchase, and it is at this point unclear. However, it would seem reasonable to suggest that parents may have been driven by a desire to experience some of the material wealth that their children were receiving (Davis and Sensenbrenner 2000: 62) report similar trends for "parental indulgence" among Shanghai adults).

One other feasible explanation would be the narrative that existed among informants, which stated that wearing similar or identical fabrics engendered particular sensations of closeness. This was most manifestly demonstrated by the existence of "family outfits" (*jiātíngzhuāng*), identical outfits available across men's, women's and children's sizes. Where there were no child cuts available the clothing was also called "lovers' outfits" (*qínrénzhuāng*). The garments were intended to be worn concurrently by family members (or unmarried couples). The shopkeeper described that the clothing was popular as it provided a "close feeling" (*qīnmì de gǎnjué*) between wearers, revealing a capacity for clothing to be conceptualized as not only expressing intimate family connections but, through the act of purchase and consumption, actually sustaining and strengthening such personal bonds. Family outfits were by no means widely worn. Some expressed distaste for the overtness of the clothing. In many ways, the "family outfit" was seen to be using a proverbial sledgehammer to crack a nut. But it does raise the possibility of denim having the potential to achieve a similar feeling of intimacy, or closeness, in a much subtler fashion. Were this supposition to be true, it would appear to corroborate Miller and Woodward's (2010) argument that denim has the capacity to express intimacy as well as globality.

Cowboy Trousers and the Closeness of Kinship

This article opened by postulating that if denim had to be considered in relationship to any single phenomenon it should be kinship, a theme that has been central to anthropological accounts of China for decades.

How did taking denim as a point of enquiry contribute to an understanding of the concept of kinship? The traditional Chinese model of kinship was portrayed as being consanguineal in nature, agnatic, stressing patrilineality, emphasized through complex kinship nomenclature categories and the corporate institution of the family. Some phenomena observed confirm elements of this system: gifting of denim from upper to lower generations constitutes the receiving of nurturance from ancestors; the widespread adoption of denim being mainly confined to the younger generation substantiates continued importance of distinguishing the generations. Concurrently, denim

also challenges the traditional system: denim was gifted from the matrilineal side rather than solely within a corporate patrilineal institution; parents owned jeans but felt uncomfortable wearing them; denim was worn by both genders with variations in styles. This evidence indicates kinship was also objectified through buying, gifting and consumption of denim, rather than being wholly dependent on biological categories dictated by "the basic facts of life … birth, conception, and death" (Fox 1967: 27). A material culture approach, accommodating individuals' relationships to denim, challenges social anthropology's conventional rendering of kinship.

Kinship is also more than, as Godelier (1998: 387) claims, mental and societal realities encompassing marriage, nomenclature, and the marking of individuals and their bodies. Looking at kinship through the lens of denim shows that such relations do not exist "as is." Rather, *kinship is created* through the minutiae of social action: the gifting of jeans from parent to child invoking traditional notions of nurturance; familial clothes shopping trips; decisions on what to wear for any given day. Multitudes of tiny gestures combine to produce the reality of being a mother, father, son, daughter, sister or brother. Denim, as much as biological fact or kinship terminology, has been shown to contribute to constructing such a reality.

Is the study of kinship, it must be then asked, useful at all? Schneider (1984: 193) dismisses kinship, arguing that it is only relevant because it has been defined by

European social scientists who use the system as the method of understanding the world around them, dryly pointing out the Nuer never told Fortes or Leach "We have patrilineal lineages …" (Schneider 1984: 4). Schneider demonstrates that not all societies have "kinship," at least in terms of social relationships connected to underlying sexual or biological fact. Godelier (1998) argues that kinship and family are not, in fact, the foundation of society and that ties based on kinship have never been enough to create corporate relations. Dousset (2007: 65) points out that Godelier's work suggests that kinship ties do not produce a society, rather, politico-religious relationships achieve this by producing and legitimatizing the sovereignty of human groups over territories and their social and materially constructed resources.

However, dismissing kinship studies altogether on the grounds of these faults runs the risk of throwing the metaphorical baby out with the bath water. This study has demonstrated that the arrangement and maintenance of family relations in Kunming remained a major concern for participants and denim was used to objectify these relationships.

Carsten (2000: 4) attempts to recast kinship as a study of "relatedness." She claims that thinking in terms of relatedness is beneficial as it allows the use of local idioms rather than pre-given definitions of what kinship is, while facilitating a move away from the inherent analytical opposition between the social and biological, on which kinship study has thus far focused. Carsten (1995: 224) illustrates this via the argument that it is only through indigenous notions of relatedness: for the Malay, she claims, living and consuming together in houses is the way in which they become kin. Carsten's description makes kinship processual, mutable and fluid, and is closer to what has been observed with denim consumption in this study.

The problem with Carsten's use of relatedness, as she notes, is that it can be used to describe either genealogical connection (and in so doing it confronts the same problem as kinship) or it can be used more generally to encompasses all relations (and is thus prone to be too unspecific). Thus, it is argued here that the study of "closeness" offers a more workable term to understand kinship. As opposed to "relatedness," "closeness" affords more primacy to an individual's immediacy (which could be understood physically, biologically, emotionally or cognitively) over that which is far away, while not rejecting the distant altogether. Importantly, such a definition also (albeit innocuously) allows the opportunity to acknowledge that very often the things *closest* to people, are exactly that: *things*. For while informants spent an important part of their lives in contact (both physically and socially) with their families and other individuals, by contrast their *entire* lives were spent in contact with objects (especially denim which was, of course, worn). These objects, as demonstrated by jeans, in addition to objectifying social relations also acted to transform informants' understanding of

kinship. Kinship as the study of "closeness" is thus advanced as it entails a requirement to consider the role objects play in everyday life and social relations.

The findings also raise the importance of the inclusion of non-denim wearers in any account of denim. If, as Miller and Woodward (2007: 336) argue, at any moment half the population of the world is clad in denim, this also entails that at any moment half the world is *not* wearing the fabric. The Chinese case shows that non-wearers played a significant role in making denim consumption the norm for those who did wear it. There are parallels here with Miller's (2010) study of denim in a small Indian town, where he argues that the adoption of jeans is dictated by caste conservatism. The difference is that in Kunming, by contrast, adoption appears much more marked by a generational conservatism.

Denim has been particularly efficacious due to its ability to insert itself into traditional notions of *yǎng* and the maintenance of kinship, enabling Kunming parents to gift it to their children in the hope their lives would be fundamentally different from their own, coupled with an awareness that an alteration in material circumstances would be necessary to achieve such a change. But denim also provoked a "kinship gulf" between children and their parents, one that parents now appeared keen to close, by purchasing and wearing denim of their own, although not without a degree of ambivalence. It is as if, having dispatched their offspring into the *Brave New World*, parents desired to follow in their progenies' footsteps, to experience some of the materiality their offspring had. Ambivalence was best reflected by the amount of parents' jeans lying inactive in wardrobes. Thus, perhaps the most remarkable discovery about denim in Kunming at the turn of the century is that it was seen as a tool that could create generational disjuncture through the most traditional of means and then later it was hoped that it would provide the solution to remove this disjuncture.

Denim has demonstrated with great subtlety an important change that has taken place within south-western Chinese society. Denim showed hope for the future of the youngest generation, a desire that through their use they could be "comfortable," in every sense of the word, not only with their family and peers but with a world "out there." Denim not only provided this opportunity, but continues to do so, day in and day out.

Notes

1. I am incredibly grateful to Professor Daniel Miller and Dr Sophie Woodward for commenting on drafts of this article. I am much obliged to Professor Yang Hui of Yunnan University who gave valuable assistance in China. This project was made possible by funding from the Economic and Social Research Council.
2. Where it has been felt to aid clarity, English translations of Mandarin Chinese are accompanied with italicized Hanyu Pinyin in parentheses.
3. The accounts were obtained during a two-month period of fieldwork in Kunming between June and July 2009. Informants' names have been replaced to protect their anonymity. All interviews with informants were conducted in standard Mandarin Chinese. I remain greatly indebted to the participants of this research who demonstrated much hospitality in allowing me into their lives.
4. For more information on the Global Denim Project visit http://www.ucl.ac.uk/global-denim-project.
5. Freedman's work concentrated on lineage in China's south-east and it should be noted that the south-west probably never quite had the same corporate dimension to kinship as Freedman's descriptions. Nevertheless, his model is included here because of its enduring influence in sinological anthropology and in this respect it provides a useful "ideal type" to balance the conclusions of this thesis against. By the same token, it should be noted that this inquiry into denim in a south-western Chinese city should not be assumed to represent China in its entirety. A wealth of anthropological studies have emphasized the heterogeneity of many aspects of Chinese life when considered on a national scale. Clothing is no different. Both my own observations and that of my informants emphasize the uniqueness of sartorial life of Kunming, both in respect of other Chinese cities and the countryside.

References

Carsten, J. 1995. "The Substance of Kinship and the Heat of the Hearth: Feeding, Personhood, and Relatedness among Malays in Pulau Langkawi." *American Ethnologist* 22(2): 223–41.

Carsten, J. 2000. "Introduction: Cultures of Relatedness." In J. Carsten (ed.) *Cultures of Relatedness: New Approaches to the Study of Kinship,* pp. 1–36. Cambridge: Cambridge University Press.

Davis, D. S. 2000. "Introduction: A Revolution in Consumption." In D. S. Davis (ed.) *The Consumer Revolution in Urban China.* Berkeley; London: University of California Press.

Davis, D. S. and Sensenbrenner, J. 2000. "Commercializing Childhood: Parental Purchases for Shanghai's Only Child." In D. S. Davis (ed.) *The Consumer Revolution in Urban China,* pp. 54–79. Berkeley, CA: University of California Press.

Diamant, N. J. 2000. *Revolutionizing the Family: Politics, Love, and Divorce in Urban and Rural China, 1949–1968.* Berkeley, CA: University of California Press.

Doolittle, J. 1866. *Social Life of the Chinese.* London: Sampson Low, Son & Marston.

Dousset, L. 2007. "'There Never Has Been Such a Thing as a Kin-Based Society': A Review Article." *Anthropological Forum: A Journal of Social Anthropology and Comparative Sociology* 17(1), 61–9.

Fong, V. L. 2004. *Only Hope: Coming of Age under China's One-child Policy.* Stanford, CA: Stanford University Press.

Fox, R. 1967. *Kinship and Marriage: An Anthropological Perspective.* Harmondsworth: Penguin.

Freedman, M. 1965. *Lineage Organization in Southeastern China.* London: University of London, Athlone Press.

Gates, H. 1987. "Money for the Gods." *Modern China* 13(3): 259–77.

Godelier, M. 1998. "Afterword: Transformation and Lines of Evolution." In M. Godelier, T. R. Trautmann and F. E. Tjon Sie Fat (eds) *Transformations of Kinship*, pp. 386–413. Washington, DC: Smithsonian Institution.

Gold, T. B. 1984. "'Just in Time!' China Battles Spiritual Pollution on the Eve of 1984." *Asian Survey* 24(9): 947–74.

He, B. 1996. "Dilemmas of Pluralist Development and Democratization in China." *Democratization* 3(3): 287–305.

Kipnis, A. 2008. "Education and the Governing of Child-Centered Relatedness." In S. Brandtstädter and G. D. Santos (eds) *Chinese Kinship: Contemporary Anthropological Perspectives,* pp. 204–22. London: Routledge.

Lévi-Strauss, C. 1969. *The Elementary Structures of Kinship.* Trans. J. H. Bell, J. von Sturmer and R. Needham. London: Eyre & Spottiswoode.

Miller, D. 2010. "The Limits of Jeans in Kannur, Kerala." In D. Miller and S. Woodward (eds) *Global Denim.* Oxford: Berg.

Miller, D. and Woodward, S. 2007. "Manifesto for a Study of Denim." *Social Anthropology* 15(3): 335–51.

Miller, D. and Woodward, S. 2010. "Introduction." In D. Miller and S. Woodward (eds) *Global Denim.* Oxford: Berg.

Morgan, L. H. 1871. *Systems of Consanguinity and Affinity of the Human Family.* Washington, DC: Smithsonian Institution.

Nien, C. 1987. *Life and Death in Shanghai.* London: Grafton.

Sautman, B. 1998. "Preferential Policies for Ethnic Minorities in China: The Case of Xinjiang." *Nationalism and Ethnic Politics* 4(1): 86–118.

Schneider, D. M. 1984. *A Critique of the Study of Kinship.* Ann Arbor, MI: University of Michigan Press.

Simmel, G. 1978. *The Philosophy of Money.* Trans. T. Bottomore and D. Frisby. London: Routledge & Kegan Paul.

Stafford, C. 1995. *The Roads of Chinese Childhood: Learning and Identification in Angang.* Cambridge: Cambridge University Press.

Stafford, C. 2000. "Chinese Patriliny and the Cycles of Yang and Laiwang." In J. Carsten (ed.) *Cultures of Relatedness: New Approaches to the Study of Kinship,* pp. 37–54. Cambridge: Cambridge University Press.

Steele, V. and Major, J. S. 1999. *China Chic: East Meets West.* New Haven, CT: Yale University Press.

Stone, L. 1997. *Kinship and Gender: An Introduction.* Boulder, CO: Westview Press.

Wang, S.-S. 1986. "The Rise and Fall of the Campaign against Spiritual Pollution in the People's Republic of China." *Asian Affairs* 13(1): 47–62.

Webb, C. 1986. "China: An Outsider's Inside View." *Asian Affairs* 17(1): 57–63.

Yan, Y. 2003. *Private Life under Socialism: Love, Intimacy and Family Change in a Chinese Village 1949–1999*. Stanford, CA: Stanford University Press.

Yan, Y. 2005. "The Individual and Transformation of Bridewealth in Rural North China." *The Journal of the Royal Anthropological Institute* 11(4): 637–58.

Zhao, X. and Belk, R. 2003. "Money to Burn: Consumption by the Dead in China." *Advances in Consumer Research* 30: 222–5.

The Denim Garment as Canvas: Exploring the Notion of Wear as a Fashion and Textile Narrative

Abstract

The markings associated with the physical wear and tear of denim garments are an integral aspect of material culture, pursued as creative concepts through deconstructed fashion approaches. For some designers a textile's heritage and the effects of time are as important as reworking silhouettes from history. While fashion is inherently forward thinking, it is the patina of age that comes from "wearing" a garment that can be integral to the designer's artistic vision. Denim garments possess unique possibilities for articulating the human form in ways that transcend the vagaries of the latest cut, through evidencing (or simulating) practices of wearing and concepts of longevity. This paper explores denim's capacity to act as a canvas for the body through analysis of a series of conceptual and commercial approaches drawn from contemporary fashion and textile designers, who have reinforced denim's origins or reinterpreted it through creative experimentation. The study is underpinned by the author's empirical research, which seeks to reveal both the recognizable and more abstract visual qualities embodied within denim as a fashion construct. Denim is evaluated as a surface for conveying complex visual signifiers relating to temporality, demonstrated through the cloth's unique facility to embody narrative and illusion.

Keywords: worn denim, deconstruction, *trompe l'oeil, wabi sabi,* patina of wear, longevity, textile narrative, laser engraving

KATHERINE TOWNSEND

Katherine Townsend PhD (2004) is a practioner and researcher in the School of Art and Design at Nottingham Trent University. Her research interests lie in the synthesizing of two- and three-dimensional textile and fashion forms, through the integration of digital and traditional technological approaches. She is currently director of MA Fashion, Knitwear and Textile Design, leads the Textile Practice research group (NTU) and is co-editor of the _Journal of Craft Research_ (Intellect).

Textile, Volume 9, Issue 1, pp. 90–107
DOI: 10.2752/175183511X12949158771554
Reprints available directly from the Publishers.
Photocopying permitted by licence only.

The Denim Garment as Canvas: Exploring the Notion of Wear as a Fashion and Textile Narrative

Introduction

This article explores the interrelationships between the surface, fabric and design of denim garments through the idea of narrative as wear. The term "wear" is used to define both the act of wearing and the consequences of wear or effect of attrition on the garment. It interrogates the parallels between the capturing of surface and drape as textile imagery, and how denim works as a material and garment structure to visualize the "aesthetic aspects of production" (Stepanova in Vinken 2005: 142).[1] The idea is informed by research into the integration of textile and garment design (Townsend 2004) and questions how new technologies are employed in synthesis with traditional design methods to visually transform the surface appearance of denim. The influence that denim has on garment spatiality is considered and defined as "architectural" at the beginning of the garment's life but it is also acknowledged that the unique transformation that takes place through wearing denim can render the same item as a "sculptural" form at a later stage of use (Townsend 2007: 119).[2]

The idiosyncratic markings associated with wearing indigo denim are described and recreated through a hybrid method of image capture combining direct printing with modeling on a mannequin.[3] The deconstructed blueprints, imbued with the memory of the fabric's manipulation, reveal the physical crafting process. The productivist elements of garment modeling such as draping, folding, pleating and pinning are used to generate unique textile narratives, achieved through a "turning outwards of the production process ... a turning-outwards of time" that empathize with the work of Martin Margiela (Vinken 2005: 142).

The article discusses how designers manipulate and exploit the fabric and surface of denim to create innovative garments by constructing visual narratives that reference both fashion and personal histories. Denim is analyzed as a canvas in relation to its conflicting characteristics, which enable it to be manhandled, marked and machined into "hard" structured shapes that yield into soft, organic forms through interaction with the human body. The strong woven structure of denim invites physical interventions, resulting in a distressed but stable material to manipulate. The dyes used to color denim respond well to washing and bleaching treatments, facilitating serendipitous patterns and chiaroscuro effects that visually contour the form of the wearer.

The visible evidence of wear and tear associated with denim through the fabric's ability to lead multiple lives is synonymous with its status as a commercial canvas. The wearing of jeans produces individual narratives that are exploited by commercial manufacturers to personalize their brands. Denim is naturally associated with product longevity but designers now intervene with the natural process of wear by applying "high and low-tech" treatments or by recycling jeans wear into *haute couture* creations. The study is particularly focused upon how different ideas of narrative relating to memory and the past are explored through the surface of denim and how this relates to and arises out of conceptual design approaches, technological interventions and practices of wearing.

Wearing Denim

While all fabrics are subject to the effects of wear and tear, denim is possibly unique for its capacity to begin life as a stiff architectural substrate but then transform over time into a softer, sculptural substrate that can be molded by the body. Its durability as a textile structure is based on its strong fiber content and warp-faced twill construction, in which a white weft or filling yarn passes under two or more, dyed warp fibers. Denim has evolved into an all-cotton "drill" fabric since the late seventeenth century when it was listed as

"serge denim" in the *Merchants Magazine,* through a variety of wool and cotton combinations including "serge de Nimes" and "jean lining," or Genoa (Alfrey-Bennett and Beattie 2008: 21). Traditionally dyed with natural indigo to make blue denims or jeans, it is now generally colored using chemical dyes in various shades of blue, black and gray for jeans-wear but can be manufactured in any shade including metallic. Washing and wearing affect the handle and appearance of the fabric: the effects of abrasion and fading of the dyed warp threads revealing more of the undyed "white" weft of the cloth. This physical and visual transmutation can have many stages, which are governed by factors such as the function of the garment, the frequency of wear, laundering and the context it is worn in.

Consumers of denim often have particular preferences about how "worn" they like their denim to be in terms of shade, texture and fabric hand. In researching this article, I interviewed twenty men and women who were all regular denim wearers aged between twenty and fifty, working in the creative industries. All were happy to provide personal accounts of how they "wear" denim, with men providing the most detailed accounts about how the "ultimate worn denim aesthetic" is achieved. Approaches included initial washing in cold water to remove starch and promote "shrink to fit"; regular washing of "new, stiff garments" in biological detergents to advance fading and flexibility; infrequent "cold" machine or hand washing of garments turned

inside out to retain depth of color/patina; the airing or dry cleaning of pieces, to preserve effects achieved through time, and the strategic abrasion of aspects of the garment to hasten the effect of wear.

The markings associated with the physical "wear and tear" of individual garments have developed as an integral aspect of denim's material culture and the effects of wearing have been explored by various designers. For Dries van Noten the concepts of age and ageing are as important as borrowing from history. While many of his designs still reference styles from the past, it was the patina of age that came from "wearing in" a garment that was integral to his early artistic vision: "One of my favourite things is a pair of old work pants that must have belonged to someone working in the chemical industry as they are covered in stains and so worn that they follow the shape of the body. In a sense, garments like these are more precious than anything else, as they have a real personal history" (Van Noten in Tucker 1999: 44).

The practice of incorporating personal histories into garments has been explored by other members of the Antwerp 6, notably Martin Margiela and Helmut Lang, as well as the British designer Hussein Chalayan. In his graduation collection The Tangent Flows (1993), Chalayan incorporated the patina of age into his fabric and garments, which he buried in the earth for six weeks allowing the rust to permeate the surface and folds of the fabric. The embracing of the signs of ageing by a significant minority of designers in the late 1990s and its acceptance as an innovative and potentially commercial concept represented a reversal of fashion being the "terrible rival" of patina (McCracken in Evans 2003: 255). Harold Koda attributed the "aesthetic of poverty" in conceptual fashion to Rei Kawakubo for Commes des Garcons, in reference to her collections from the early 1980s, which drew upon the principles of Japanese *wabi sabi* by attributing "superior value, based on enlightened recognition, to the flawed artefact and to poor materials" (Evans 2003: 256).

Not Made by Hand

The relationship between patina and denim is primarily derived from its introduction as a durable work wear fabric, typically in the form of farm workers' smocks in East Anglia, UK and jeans in the Mid-West of America from the mid-nineteenth century (Alfrey-Bennett

Figure 1
Levi's 501 trucker jacket and jeans 1982–95. Owned and photographed by Ian Cutmore.

and Beattie 2008: 23). The marks of wear made by the bodies of hard-working physical laborers resulted in the customization of denim, transforming it from "serviceable, affordable clothing" into something much more unique. Traditionally woven denim still possesses an almost unrivalled facility to "to stick, cling to"[4] or be shaped through wear to an individual's physique. Indigo-dyed denim is particularly susceptible to fading and marking, each set of creases, providing evidence of the cloth's manipulation through repeated patterns of movement.

The ways in which the body leaves its mark on another material are particularly significant in the case of denim but is not unique to it. Two well known examples of this phenomenon are the Turin Shroud and Veronica's Cloth, known in Greek as *archeiropoietos*, meaning "not made by hand" (Kuryluk 1991: 1). The Turin Shroud is imbued with the impression of a male figure, believed to be Christ and created through the chemical reaction of the body's decomposition with the cloth. The suggestion of the male form is overlaid with inverted diamond patterns caused by the folding of the shroud over time. The image has the appearance of a photographic negative or X-ray, the lighter shades denoting the body's contact with the shroud.

In his essay Lumbar Thought (1976), Umberto Eco discusses the intimacy of wearing denim, how the restrictive characteristics of tight jeans not only physically shape his form, but his thoughts, presenting a semiotic coding that affects his behavior (Eco 1986). The facility for fitted denim garments to act

as an exoskeleton is reliant on the fabric conforming to an individual's particular body shape as it is worn and laundered; shrinking and stretching each time it is washed and reworn (Figure 1). Over time denim not only carries the impression of the wearer, but evidence of their personality. Gordon (2009: 334) uses the term "scars" to describe the stains, rips, frayed areas and patches, associated with remembered events and experiences, reinforcing the metaphor of denim as a "second skin," as illustrated in Figure 2. The signs of wear resulting from the idiosyncratic relationship between the body and denim, through repeated activity and creasing are a visual trace of the body's actions, perceived by some as an irreplaceable "perfect point" of wear:

> *I have had a Red Ear Paul Smith jacket for 6/7 years which has only been dry cleaned twice and has been worn I would say at least twice a week until now—it is on the path of ceasing to exist. I could never throw it away. I am in a dilemma do I patch it or let it fade away to nothing with grace? This jacket has become my skin; the combination of the designers cut, my body and my actions on it and in it, make it unique.* (Interview with artist Wolfgang Buttress, Nottingham, December 11, 2009)

Commerce and Denim

The commercialization of patina as surface design for denim garments stems from its introduction as work wear in California by Levi Strauss in

the 1850s.[5] Artists recognized the value of denim as a cloth that could be individualized through wear from the early twentieth century when it was adopted as an early form of anti-fashion (Gordon 2009: 331). In the 1930s Levi's began to exploit denim's early romantic associations with gold prospectors and cowboys, transforming the laborers' uniform and its associated hard-wearing properties into a desirable fashion item. These links were reinforced by the availability of jeans as part of welfare packages in the Great Depression and the issuing of Lee's Union All and Levi's 501 jeans to American armed forces in the First and Second World Wars. By the 1960s, protestors against the Vietnam conflict redefined jeans as a visible symbol of disenfranchised youth; the act of wearing becoming a way of undermining both mainstream politics and the plastic veneer of seasonal fashion (Gordon 2009: 332; Huiguang 2007: 336).

In contemporary fashion, fabrication techniques are commonly applied to integrate the "effects of time" into denim to attach the material qualities and philosophical meanings that consumers are increasingly searching for. The commercial jeans wear industry has been strongly influenced by vintage trends and applies signifiers of "authenticity" and "sustainability" to market products effectively. For example, Levi's is currently advertising its Vintage 1947 501 Rigid Jeans: "made on original looms, the denim will feel stiff at first but after a few days will soften and mould to your body shape. Wear your jeans for six months

Figure 2
Sleeve of Paul Smith Red Ear denim
jacket 2003–10; photograph by
Wolfgang Buttress.

before washing them, preferably by hand" (www. Levi's.com, accessed January 10, 2010).

The description references some of the key characteristics attributed to the quality and longevity of worn denim. The strap-line for another vintage style, the 1890 XX501 Buried Wrath Jeans claims "extreme vintage status," complete with "rust staining on the knees and pocket, as if the garment has lived life on a hard-working man." The style is redolent of the soiled and tattered Dust Storm series of pre-washed, warm-cast jeans launched in 1986 (Huiguang 2007: 114). Levi's First Standard 10th Blast Jeans celebrate the tenth birthday of Engineered Jeans, through "a very limited 99 pairs of hand painted anniversary jeans," featuring a carefully engineered design simulating the effect of abstract expressionist painting and bleach marks. The style is similar to the Japanese "crush" processing style introduced by Sweet Camel, which combines paint staining and aperture boring (Huiguang 2007: 329).

Other jean brands that could be discussed in relation to their brand longevity are Lee (1889), Wrangler (1904) and Lee Cooper (1908). The French designer label Girbaud, founded in 1964, is notable for its aim to reflect humanitarian and conceptual ideals through the cut, fabric and finishing of its garments and was one of the first companies to change the look of its jeans by stonewashing them in 1965. The commercialization of worn and faded looks began in 1969 with the use of pre-bleached denim with entrepreneurial companies offering laundering and treatment services on a bespoke basis. Guess Inc was one of the first companies, along with Lee, to exploit the pre-washed look during the 1980s, using a twelve-hour stonewashing method that gave the jeans the appearance of sun-bleached denim. The time-consuming process was replaced with the chemical technique of acid washing, resulting in a snow-washed effect that together with slicing and fraying came to define designer denim at this time. Initially, commentators criticized these approaches as "faddish dishonesty" that denied the consumer or "person within" the opportunity to create a "life mould" of themselves in denim (Berendt, in Gordon 2009: 337).

Calvin Klein (1968), Diesel (1978), DKNY (1988) and Dolce and Gabbana (1996) are also notable for their body defining cut, surface treatments and striking advertising campaigns relating to the personalization and sexualization of denim. Diesel is one of the most proactive companies in terms of aesthetic ageing treatments, creating the effects of "destruction, damage, filth and mould" by using various techno-chemical systems including "Flow Dye" and "Drift Ice Dye" (Huiguang 2007: 329). DSquared2, G-Star Raw, Energie, Replay, APC, For All Mankind, Nudie and Japanese brands Edwin and Kato represent some of the most innovative new labels. Nudie are notable for their 100 percent sustainable credentials through the use of use of Japanese hand looms, indigo plant dyes, natural cellulosic washing and bleaching in conjunction with sustainable denim.

Treatment of the surface and structure of denim to create "authentic" effects is now achieved at all levels of the market using any manner of high or low technologies. Some jeans wear companies use a combination of hand sanders and grinders on perfect jeans, manufactured in China, to simulate the effects of deterioration as a form of bespoke surface detailing. Digital cutting technology is employed to create distressed characteristics by rupturing the fabric with strategically placed/frayed slashes, crosses and squares, resulting in a tailor made "worn" look, as illustrated by Levi's Slim cut (2009).

The tension between how the outer and inner layer of denim are rendered to create commercial fashion narratives has been facilitated by the composition of the canvas-like cloth. Laser cutting is now often employed, sometimes in conjunction with bleaching and printing, to create sophisticated, multi-layered designs. When washed, laser-cut denim is liable to fray but cleaner cutting can be achieved by reinforcing the fabric. A more viable possibility is "engraving" whereby the laser cutter is adjusted to etch the top/dyed (weft) surface of the denim to reveal the lighter (warp) backing, making the pattern appear inverted and extremely effective, as illustrated in Figure 3 (interview with Sue Turton, Laser cutting designer/technician, Nottingham Trent University, December 10, 2009). The use of hand and/or digital technologies to create ideas of authenticity presents an interesting paradox: that is, the faking of a garment's personal history.

The Garment as Canvas and Denim as Surface

The term "garment as canvas" has been used in earlier research to categorize printed (or embellished) garments interpreted as three-dimensional (3D) canvases (Townsend 2008). These pieces can be painterly, graphic, designed to be thought provoking or to convey concepts that question the intersection between art and fashion. Caroline Broadhead's Web (1989)[6] and Martin Margiela's dresses injected with mold spores from the "9/4/1615" exhibition (1997)[7] provide examples of conceptual garments that inspired the author's methodology for creating 3D printed canvases or "cyanoforms." The capturing of pinned and wrapped cloth shapes using the cyanotype process resulted in indigo dyed textiles that were redolent of the surfaces of worn denim garments, appearing to have evolved over time. The recording of the tension between the surface and draping qualities of the fabrics resulting in *trompe l'oeil*

Figure 3
Laser etched design on denim swatch by Sue Turton, designed by Jason Holroyd (2009).

impressions of the narrative of wear on cloth (Figure 4).

"Canvas" is a term that has also been associated with denim, from its origins as a strong canvas cloth for tents to its ready constitution as a blank surface upon which meanings can be created through wear and personalization. In the exhibition Denim: The Fabric of our Lives, Alfrey-Bennett and Beattie (2008: 26) refer to the denim canvas as:

> *An ideal sub-stratum for surface embroidery such as an elegant Louboutin high heeled shoe, a potent symbol of exaggerated femininity that positions denim just about as far as it can be removed from its masculine work-wear identity.*

Pieces in the exhibition illustrated how denim has been used literally as a canvas through mixed media techniques, such as printing, hand painting and embroidery, applied to all or key aspects of garments as personal customization.

The exhibition also showcased surreal statements by fashion artists such as Issey Miyake who transposed a life-size photographic print of a straight denim skirt onto a Pleats Please version and Jean-Charles de Castelbajac who created a dress printed with the stitch outlines of jeans (Alfrey-Bennett and Beattie 2008: 52).

The *haute couture* garments presented in the Denim exhibition included interpretations by Vivienne Westwood, Hussein Chalayan and Christian Lacroix. Westwood's two-piece suits explored denim's oppositional fabric qualities of fine/coarse and feminine/masculine through the transposing of *trompe l'oeil* lace prints. Hussein Chalayan's Echoform collection (1999/2000) used a computer-animated film of a series of near-identical denim dresses that played with principles of construction and deconstruction through adding and removing stitching and pocket detailing. Each dress echoed the details

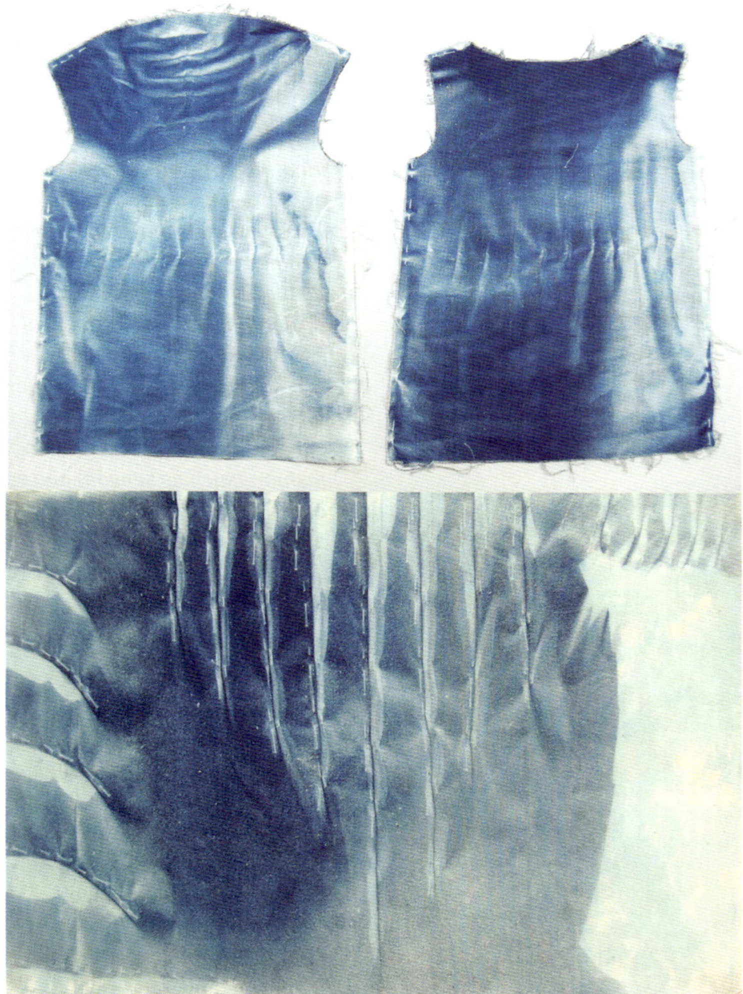

Figure 4
Katherine Townsend (2001) Shadow Tunic and Pin Wrap from Cyanoform Series 3, cyanotype on calico.

of the previous model using the garment as a metaphor for memory and loss (Evans 2003: 57–9). Christian Lacroix's denim ball gown challenged the notion of denim's utilitarian heritage by reworking it into a fantasy structure where seam stitching was applied as boning to contour the waist and denim jackets were attached as alternative panniers. The dress is a contradiction—Lacroix's bespoke embroidery replaced with the pragmatic embellishments of production: metal rivets, double-stitching and leather patches. However, it was the faded elements of the garment that were most arresting; how could a ball gown have had so many previous owners and lives? Hill (2009) articulates the viewers' confusion: "How do we understand a cloth that possesses such seemingly paradoxical qualities: a fabric that is identified with both rebellion and conformity; that is unyielding yet moulds to the body; a cloth that is ubiquitous yet personal; an everyman fabric that is used within *haute couture*?"

Design Interventions: The Manipulation of the Surface

Historically, it is garments, as opposed to textiles, which have been analyzed as cultural signifiers; the silhouette and detailing reflecting a particular set of socio-political circumstances.

In The Fashion System (1983)[8] Barthes focuses on the deconstruction of fashion but also acknowledges textiles as "vital signifiers" of meaning.

> Identified by Barthes as one of the "vestimentary features" which can be used to construct and deconstruct meaning from fashion, fabric is discussed throughout the text in terms of its signified meaning and how it is combined with other signifiers internal to fashion (such as cut and drape) and external to fashion (such as season, place and situation) to create further meaning. (Andrew 2008: 34)

The consideration of textile semantics and the idea of denim being classified as a "vital signifier" of meaning is an interesting but problematic proposition. The interrelationship between the cut and drape of a denim garment makes it difficult to isolate and evaluate the surface of the textile in terms of "language." Reducing denim to language fails to appreciate its complex materiality both as a textile and garment construct. The self-patterning of denim that occurs over time provides a narrative of wear that signifies an individual's past actions, which can only be translated or read by the wearer, close family members, or the textile literate.

Denim garments are structured and defined by their edges, which evidence wear in a different way from the softer planes of the clothing. The strength of the cloth requires specific manufacturing and finishing techniques. The "four hallmarks of Levi's 501 jeans": copper rivets, Arcurate pocket stitching, leather patch and red tabs, have been interpreted by most jeans manufacturers along with the prerequisite double-stitched seams and hems (Huiguang 2007: 101). These signs of production are inherent to denim's vocabulary, so the surface is not only the fabric as it is woven or treated but how it is constructed. The "lexis of production" is made visible on denim, the stitches and fasteners viewed as forms of post-fashion decorative embellishment (Vinken 2005: 142).

Elsa Schiaparelli's Tear Dress (1937) provides an important example of the use of fabric constructs as decoration.[9] The patterning depicted on the Tear Dress has been variously described as "torn flesh" and "rags," and provides an early example of the employment of trompe l'oeil images to simulate the physical characteristics of fabric. Graphic software and inkjet printing technology have enabled designers to exploit surreal concepts by transposing images of textile textures onto disparate qualities. Figure 5 illustrates how the effect of worn indigo denim can be simulated through the strategic digital manipulation of tonal images of pleats and folds to suggest multi-directional rhythms of cloth that radiate from invisible seams and openings, which could not be crafted manually.

The Tear Dress is considered as inspiration for Vivienne Westwood's Cut and Slash (1991) collection, which physically challenged the surface of denim by employing the seventeenth-century technique of slashing (Wilcox 2004: 117).[10]

Figure 5
Katherine Townsend (2009)
Reconfigured section of Moon Pleat
Skirt (2004).

Westwood also used "destroyed" effects in Tied to the Mast (1998), where the advertising campaign based on Gericault's Raft of the Medusa (1819) showed models in denim separates that appeared to have been weathered by the salt water and storm. The "cruel and unusual treatment of fabrics" is central to the Japanese concept of *boro boro,* explored by Nuno Corporation and which translates as: "ragged, torn, worn-out, dilapidated" (Hodges 1997). The company's director, Reiko Sudo, has worked with Issey Miyake and Rei Kawakubo, to create garments that exploit the fabric's surface to suggest concepts and histories. This resonates with Baudrillard's claim, of key importance here, relating to the radical material illusion of the world and its unexpected effects. Things have become so accelerated that processes are no longer inscribed in a linear temporality, in a linear unfolding of history (Baudrillard 2000: 177).

Denim's inherent quality of recording temporal effects throughout different stages of wear enables a garment to be aesthetically assessed by both wearer and viewer. Designers constantly manipulate this idiosyncratic characteristic by disrupting the linear progression of time. Alexander McQueen's Dante

Autumn/Winter 1996/97 collection drew details from the fourteenth century to reflect the suffering of religious war by using uneasy images[11] on luxurious fabrics, fine boning and military embroidery, contrasted with frayed, patch-worked and bleached dyed denim, used symbolically to reinforce the ravages of conflict (www.vam.co.uk, accessed February 9, 2010). Chloe's Spring/Summer 2010 collection insinuates the passage of time through denim separates treated to look as if pockets and patches have been removed from a naturally bleached garment, revealing darker indigo shapes beneath (www.vogue.co.uk, accessed March 5, 2010).[12]

Martin Margiela: Stealing Time

The distressed denim aesthetic explored throughout this article has been strongly influenced by a deconstructed fashion approach. Referred to by Evans (2003: 149) as "dereliction," this genre was initiated in the 1980s by Japanese designers, notably Rei Kawakubo, and developed by a small but significant group of European designers, particularly Martin Margiela.

> *Martin Margiela's 'new materials' were fashion detritus when he started with them; second-hand or army surplus is the commodity form with the lowest exchange value in the fashion system. Like a nineteenth century rag-picker, who gathered scraps for recycling, Margiela converted low-status second-hand clothing into the high status of a unique fashion piece.* (Evans 2003: 149)

Although Margiela has not used denim extensively in his collections, his work has clear implications and resonances with the wider issues considered so far. I will therefore draw an analogy between Margiela's practices and how designers work with denim. His role as the "Golden Dustman" of fashion has resulted in some memorable treatments that have permeated the psychology of fashion (Evans 1998). During the late 1990s, Margiela's collections regularly featured items of second-hand clothing, transformed with a print or re-made through a unique process of "deconstruction and reproduction" (Evans 1998: 75). In 1997 he collaborated with microbiologists to create the installation "9/4/1615," where conceptual garments were treated with mold spores, cultivated on the garments to form their embellishment. The spores became part of the fabric, impregnating the fibers, just as washing, staining, tearing affects the surface and structure of denim. In Spring/Summer 2001 he used an outsized mannequin found in a street in Italy to model a collection at over 150 percent "normal," or standard size. The pieces included a pair of faded, distressed jeans at 200 percent, which were doubled around the model's waist, appearing more as a long, wrapped skirt than trousers. The garments challenged the notion of standardized sizing and were in complete opposition to the fitted styles of commercial jeans brands.

At the Maison Martin Margiela "20" exhibition (2008), the concept of *trompe l'oeil* and architectural devices such as open doors leading to windows beyond, introduced the audience to the artist's conceptual oeuvre. *Trompe l'oeil* is central to many of Margiela's collections and

Figure 6
Martin Margiela, Printed dress from
Spring/Summer 1998. Photo taken by
the author at Maison Martin Margiela
"20," MoMu, Antwerp, 2008.

it is this style of visual manipulation and surfacing techniques that have been so influential in terms of this study. For Spring/Summer 1996, photographs of a vintage dress lining were transfer printed onto light and fluid fabrics and made into simple dress constructions. The *trompe l'oeil* creases, seams, facings and fastenings convince the viewer of the existence of a much more complex garment through the illusion of the inside of a dress on the outside of another. As shown in Figure 6, although made of silky fabric, the printed effect and coloration suggest parallels with denim. The silver foiled vintage jeans shown in Figure 7 illustrate another way in which Margiela incorporates of the passage of time into his fabrics and garments. Here the process of age and decay is frozen within the garment by the layer of ink "a snapshot in the unstoppable passing of time and history" (Debo 2008: 9).

In her essay, "Time and Body," the curator of the exhibition Kaat Debo (2008) analyzes the importance of these two aspects within the conceptualization of the Maison Martin Margiela aesthetic:

> *The concept of time can be interpreted in various ways: as the duration—or durée—that is expressed through the use of certain fabrics and objects attesting to the passage of time and the process of ageing; time in the guise of history of fashion; and finally, time as referring to the history of the garment itself, which is made visible through the externalisation of the production process.*

It is this "making visible" of a garment's history, either through

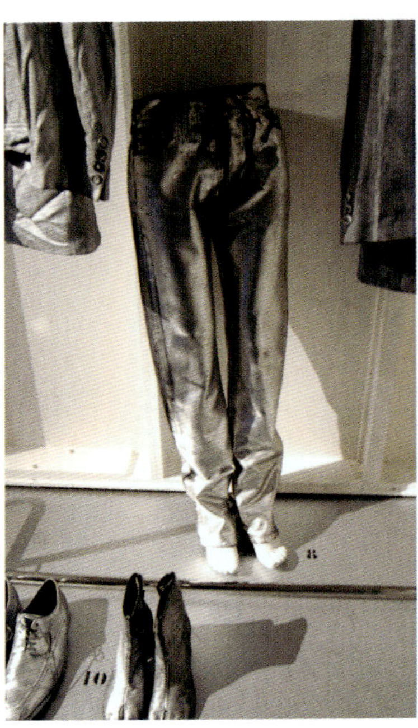

Figure 7
Martin Margiela: Silver foiled vintage jeans, jackets and shoes S/S 2003. Photograph taken by the author at Maison Martin Margiela "20," MoMu, Antwerp, 2008.

found or created histories, that is so fundamental to Margiela's legacy and contemporary denim textiles. Denim garments visualize their production through a historical referencing system of design details: zips, rivets, top stitching, belt loops, patch pockets double-stitched seams. Denim fabric evidences the life lived by the garment and its wearer through a very different set of visual codes: fading, staining, tearing, fraying, discoloration and partial disintegration.

Conclusion

Denim garments are now pre-washed, polished and shaped by designers making it more challenging for individuals to customize their clothing through wear. Despite the proliferation of aesthetically aged and treated denim products on the market, consumers still have strong preferences as to how they wear denim and how they achieve a perfect point of wear. The surface marks acquired by denim through everyday life are not perceived as flaws but often as scars, reinforcing the metaphor of cloth as a vehicle for personal narratives. It is perhaps for this reason that, when garments reach a pivotal stage of aesthetic perfection, some wearers strive to conserve them in a similar way to bespoke or *haute couture* items.

The markings associated with the physical "wear and tear" of individual garments have been exploited by the commercial jeans industry and explored conceptually by key fashion designers. The influence of Martin Margiela, Rei Kawakubo and Reiko Sudo has led to a more theoretical approach to denim. The deconstruction of denim has resulted in creatively destructive approaches that have raised awareness of Eastern philosophies, which recognize a different beauty in the flawed artifact.

The signs of wear resulting from the idiosyncratic relationship between the body and denim are not made by hand but are formed through a process of iteration resulting in a visual trace of the body's actions permeating the cloth. Commerce constantly seeks to simulate this through the application of cutting edge and traditional technologies. Today's consumers seek product authenticity in terms of cut, surface design, detailing and

increasingly the provenance of the materials and processes. Higher quality, traditionally woven denim can withstand multiple levels of treatments, adding layers of value to a garment. Strategic dyeing and laser etching treatments introduce unique brand signifiers, allowing consumers to "buy-in" as opposed to "wear-in" their jeans.

Denim garments can be viewed as physical and conceptual canvases. This relates to the woven construction of the cotton drill, which can absorb wet and dry media applications and will not disintegrate when cut. The flexibility and strength of the cloth makes it hard wearing, allowing for it to be worn, reworn and recycled. Vintage denim is valued for the patina of age and unique surface designs it carries. Denim is a staple of each new season's collection so, although silhouettes and treatments change, the fabric is timeless.

Various designers and artists have experimented with denim garments as canvases to convey meanings belonging to and beyond fashion. Hussein Chalayan's Echoform dress collection A/W 1999/2000 played with principles of production through animated construction and deconstruction of stitched details. The work underpinned Stepanova's belief in seaming and stitching as decoration while symbolizing concepts of memory and loss. Denim's design vocabulary is inextricably linked to its manufacture. Jeans are fashioned from eleven components, in particular stages that are made visible on denim. The production of jeans still evidences a linear unfolding of history. Denim can

be inscribed by the marks of temporality, enabling it to hold narratives that few other textiles can accommodate.

Martin Margiela's practice of incorporating histories of fabric, garment and time into his work raises interesting parallels with contemporary denim production. His emphasis on the value of craft through the externalization of the production process and the capturing of patina provides fashion with the principles of longevity that should be emulated if denim is to retain its potential beauty as a cloth and authenticity as a vehicle for fashion and textile narratives.

Notes

1. In "The dress of today is the industrial dress" (1923) Vivara Stepanova stated that "Aesthetic aspects must be replaced by the process of sewing itself."

2. The "architectural" and "sculptural" archetypal garment shapes defined in Townsend (2007) are developed from observations of the practice of the Constructivist artist Luibov Popova, in Adaskina and Sarabianov (1990: 303).

3. The simultaneous design method applied in the research was inspired by Sonia Delaunay's *tissue simultané* and developed as a 3D process for designing printed garments using blueprinting in conjunction with manual modeling and CAD/CAM technology as discussed in Townsend (2004: Chapter 5).

4. The word "cloth" is of Germanic origin, appearing

in *Kleid* (dress) and *Kleidung* (clothing), derived from the root *kli-* "to stick" or "to cling to," making "cloth," "that which clings to the body" (Kuryluk 1991: 179).

5. The California Gold Rush of 1849 resulted in a growing population of immigrant gold prospectors, known as the "'49ers" who needed strong and inexpensive workwear. Levi Strauss & Co was founded in 1850 and by 1855 it was manufacturing Waist High Overalls and pantaloons using the duck and sail cloth originally intended for tents and covered wagons. In 1873 Levi Strauss & Co and Jacob Davis jointly patented Davis's invention of metal rivets used to reinforce stress points in the overalls (Huiguang 2007: 15–24).

6. See De Givry (1998) for more details.

7. "9/4/1615," Museum Van Beuningen, Rotterdam, 1997, featured in Evans (2003).

8. The Fashion System was originally published in 1967 in France as Systeme de la Mode.

9. The visual qualities of deconstruction presented through this dress, have been analyzed by Martin (1988) as visual metaphors for the destructive political atmosphere of the Spanish Civil War and spread of Fascism throughout Europe. The piece is also credited as inspiration for later physically distressed pieces such as Rei Kawakubo's Lace Sweater (1982) and Vivienne Westwood's ripped denim styles of the 1990s (Steele 1997).

10. "The effect was achieved in a variety of ways: the large slashes were hand-cut, while the smaller, regular cuts were made using a broderie anglaise programme in which embroidered sections were cut, but the embroidery itself omitted" (Wilcox 2004:117).

11. The images were by the photographer Don McCullin.

12. The March 2010 issue of *Vogue* featured an article about Denim written by acting editor, Alexa Chung who stated: "Denim is a symbol of youth, sex, rebellion and, most essentially, America."

References

Adaskina, N. and Sarabianov, D. 1990. *Liubov Popova*, London: Thames & Hudson.

Alfrey-Bennett, P. and Beattie, V. 2008. *Denim: The Fabric of our Lives*, Exhibition catalog, Hub. Sleaford: National Centre for Craft and Design.

Andrew, S. 2008. "Textile Semantics: Considering a Communication-based Reading of Textiles." *Textile* 6(1): 32–65.

Barthes, R. 1983. *The Fashion System*. Trans. M. Ward and R. Howard. New York: Hill & Wang.

Baudrillard, J. 2000. "The Murder of the Real." In J. Witwer (ed.) *The Vital Illusion*. New York: Colombia University Press.

Debo, K. 2008. *Maison Martin Margiela "20" The Exhibition*. Essay in exhibition catalogue, MoMu, Antwerp.

De Givry, V. 1998. *Art and Mode: L'inspiration artistique des creators de mode.* Paris: Editions du Regard.

Eco, U. 1986. "Lumbar Thought." In *Travels in Hyperreality*, Translated by William Weaver. San Diego, CA: Harcourt Brace & Co.

Evans, C. 1998. "Martin Margiela: The Golden Dustman." *Fashion Theory* 2(1): 73–94.

Evans, C. 2003. *Fashion at the Edge.* New Haven, CT: Yale University Press.

Gordon, B. 2009. "American Denim: Blue Jeans and their Multiple Layers of Meaning." In P. McNeil and V. Karaminas (eds) *The Men's Fashion Reader*, pp. 331–40. Oxford: Berg.

Kuryluk, E. 1991. "Veronica and Her Cloth: History, Symbolism, and Structure of a 'True' Image." Oxford: Blackwell.

Hill, J. 2009. "Exhibition Review, Denim: The Fabric of our Lives." *Textile* 7(1): 98–105.

Hodges, R. 1997. "Boro Boro: Cruel and Unusual Treatment of Fabrics." Washington, DC: The Textile Museum Shop.

Huiguang, Z. 2007 *Delirious Denim.* London: Southbank Publishing.

Martin, R. 1988. *Fashion and Surrealism.* London: Thames & Hudson

McNeil, P. and Karaminas, V. (eds). 2009. *The Men's Fashion Reader.* Oxford: Berg.

Steele, V. 1997. "Fifty Years of Fashion: New Look to Now." New Haven, CT and London: Yale University Press.

Stepanova, V. 1923. "Kostyum sevodnyashnevo dnya— Prozodezhda." ("The Costume of Today—Production Clothing.") *LEF* 2: 65–8

Townsend, K. 2004. "Transforming Shape." PhD thesis, Nottingham Trent University.

Townsend, K. 2007. "The Spatial Garment, Exhibition and Essay." In *New Craft—Future Voices*, Cooper Gallery, Duncan of Jordanstone College of Art and Design, University of Dundee, July 4– August 3, 2007, pp. 118–23.

Townsend, K. 2008. "On the Dress She Wears a (Printed) Body." *The Body: Connections with Fashion*, Tenth Annual Conference for the International Foundation of Fashion Technology Institutes (IFFTI), RMIT Melbourne, Australia, 8–9 March.

Tucker, A. 1999. *Dries Van Noten: Shape, Print and Fabric.* London: Thames & Hudson.

Vinken, B. 2005. "Martin Margiela: Signs and Time." In *Fashion Zeitgeist: Trends and Cycles in the Fashion System.* Trans. Mark Hewson. Oxford: Berg.

Wilcox, C. 2004. *Vivienne Westwood.* London: V & A Publishing.

Exhibition Review

*Beyond Bloomsbury: Designs of the
Omega Workshop 1913–19*

Exhibition Review
Beyond Bloomsbury: Designs of the Omega Workshop 1913–19

The Courtauld Gallery, London, June 18–September 20, 2009

"Beyond Bloomsbury: Designs of the Omega Workshop 1913–19" is an apt title for this exhibition of Omega textile designs, which was indeed shown just beyond Bloomsbury in the Courtauld Gallery, Somerset House on The Strand, London. The "Omega workshop" was set up as a creative enterprise by Roger Fry, Vanessa Bell and Duncan Grant of the Bloomsbury Group[1] in an inconspicuous townhouse, 33 Fitzroy Square, Bloomsbury, London. The domestic interiors were their shop, gallery, workspace and offices from 1913 to 1919, a period that included the First World War.

This timely exhibition is a gentle reminder that, during wartime as during a recession, fashioning designs of bright and colorful textiles can lift one's spirits and that the application of textile designs to domestic interiors reinforces the relationship between arts and crafts, reflecting boundaries that are as blurred today as they were 100 years ago.

> *It is time the spirit of fun was introduced into Furniture and into Fabrics. We have suffered far too long from the dull and stupidly serious.* (Roger Fry 1913)[2]

As an Omega client you would have stepped through the door of the townhouse into a creative world, where you could see and meet the artists at work, in the two adjacent showrooms on the ground floor, two workshop rooms on the first floor and above that the Omega offices. The "open studio" feel (see Figure 1) about the Omega workshop had clearly been influenced by Ruskin's[3] writings, which contributed to the Omega's unique and successful "shopping"

REVIEWED BY
LUCY GUNDRY

Lucy Gundry is a doctoral research student at the Royal College of Art and an associate lecturer in textile theory at University of the Arts, London. Her work investigates the relationship between dress, the body and touch in the contemporary exhibition space.

Textile, Volume 9, Issue 1, pp. 108–119
DOI: 10.2752/175183511X12949158771590
Reprints available directly from the Publishers.
Photocopying permitted by licence only.

Figure 1
Roger Fry in the Omega Workshops,
c. 1913. Published in Richard Shone,
Bloomsbury Portraits: Vanessa Bell,
Duncan Grant, and their Circle (Oxford:
Phaidon, 1976).

experience: "The desire of the heart is also the light of the eyes. No scene is continually and untiringly loved, but one rich by joyful human labour [...]" (Ruskin 2005: 76).

The exhibition is spread across two adjacent gallery spaces off the central spiral staircase, which guides us up the eighteenth-century palace of Somerset House. We enter through a door into the first of the gallery spaces, moving onto a second smaller gallery space, which is domestically elegant and intimate, akin to 33 Fitzroy Square, but there is no natural light.

At 33 Fitzroy Square, the Omega workshop sign was hung unassumingly with its handmade Greek "Ω" symbol above the outside entrance (see Figure 2). Interestingly, in the exhibition the original Omega sign is present and also hung unassumingly but above the doorway into the second smaller exhibition room. In the original setting, however, the sign was flanked by painted dancers set into the façade of the

Figure 2
Omega Workshops (Duncan Grant),
Signboard, 1915, Oil on wood with metal
studs, 104.1 × 63.2 cm, The Victoria and
Albert Museum, London.

townhouse (see Figure 3)—perhaps the exhibition might have reflected the sign's original purpose more successfully had it been positioned above the exhibition entrance.

All five of the Omega artists (Vanessa Bell, Duncan Grant, Wyndham Lewis, Frederick Etchells and French sculptor Henri Gaudier-Brzesha) were brought together by Fry because of their personal vision, however individual authorship of their designs was sacrificed under the unity of the workshop and the "Ω" symbol.

This became an issue for one particular artist, Wyndham Lewis, who railed against Fry's Quaker[4] philosophy, objecting to the anonymity of his contribution to the Ideal Home exhibition of 1913. He walked out after only three months. Lewis went on to form the arguably more successful "Vorticist" movement, which was a patriotic movement (closely related to Futurism)[5] in political opposition to Fry's pacifism.

Although some of the dissention around the Omega

Figure 3
Entrance to 33 Fitzroy Square.
Published in A.T. Bolton, "The
Architecture of Robert and James
Adam (1758–94)." *Country Life*, 1922.

philosophy was latterly rectified
by "attributing" designs to
specific artists, as we see in
the exhibition labeling, this of
course undermines the Omega
philosophy. Nevertheless, as
visitors to the exhibition, we are
pleased to discover which designs
are "attributed" to which artists.

Fry was a ceramicist, painter
and entrepreneur and had
international connections. The

Figure 4
Omega Workshops, Amenophis,
1913. Designed by Roger Fry. Made in
France. Printed linen, 60.2 × 78.2 cm.
Victoria and Albert Museum, London.
Given by Margaret Bulley 1934.

Figure 5
Omega Workshops, White, 1913.
Design attributed to Vanessa Bell.
Made in France. Printed linen,
62.2 × 78.3 cm. Victoria and
Albert Museum, London. Given
by Roger Fry 1913.

Figure 6
Omega Workshops, Mechtilde, 1913. Printed linen. Made in France. Manchester
City Art Gallery.

workshops were patronized by a well-connected elite, and even royalty: "Alongside Virginia Woolf [...] Maud Cunard, George Bernard Shaw and Princess Lichnowsky, wife of the Imperial German Ambassador to the Court of St James's 1912–14" (Levitt and Whitten 2009).[6] Other Omega visitors were contemporary minded and international. Indeed at the time "The shop and its products were advertised in the style of art exhibitions" (Levitt and Whitten 2009), which would have appealed to the Omega audiences of the time as much as to the gallery visitors of today.

It also seems ironic that the six designs, launched by the Omega workshop in 1913, were each "given" random names (rather than the names of the artists) by Princess Mechtilde Lichnowsky on the opening night, including one she named after herself. Others related to those who were loosely involved with the workshop, for example: "Margery" who was Fry's favorite sister and "Maud" who was Lady Maud Cunard, a regular client. Today these names sit above the "attributed" artist name in the labeling of the exhibition pieces and run down the far left hand side of the gallery. They are as follows:

- "Amenophis"—attributed to Roger Fry (see Figure 4);
- "Margery"—attributed to Duncan Grant;
- "White"—attributed to Vanessa Bell (see Figure 5);
- "Maud"—attributed to Vanessa Bell;
- "Mechtilde"—attributed to Frederick Etchells (see Figure 6);

Figure 7
Omega Workshops, Pamela, 1913.
Printed linen. Made in France.
Manchester City Art Gallery.

- "Pamela"—attributed to Duncan Grant (see Figure 7).

It is thought that the Omega artists were influenced by the "decorative unity" of Henri Matisse, Fauvism[7] and influences deriving from "Arts & Crafts." The French Fauves and Matisse inspired strong color, fluid lines painted directly onto canvas, creating a bright aesthetic to counteract the dull tones of British designs. These designs not only went on to influence British textiles in the early part of the twentieth century but continued to translate successfully into twenty-first century design, spanning a whole century of timeless style.

The Omega workshop combined artists, designers and craftsmen as Fry had intended, breaking down the boundaries between fine and decorative arts and introducing contemporary art into domestic interiors. It pioneered collaborations, which are still contentious today, between the fine and decorative arts by applying their fabric designs to furniture, dress and interiors including screens and ceramics.

In the exhibition we see a figurative screen by Vanessa Bell and a collection of Fry's black and white ceramic plates in the second room along with the "Lily Pond" table and matching cupboard, which was decorated with brightly colored paint poured directly onto the wooden surface in pools and allowed to dry as it formed (see Figure 8). The artists painted their pieces, tried out different color ways as part of a multiple process, then translated these into scaled sections on paper in mirror image, so their designs could be read by professional craftsmen. However there are no examples of actual interiors in the exhibition, which I feel could have gone some way to reinventing the Omega spirit.

Interestingly, though, some of the designs were drawn in reverse, as they would have gone

Figure 8
Omega Workshops (Duncan Grant),
Four-fold screen with lily pond design,
1913–14. Oil on wood, 181.6 × 242.4 cm.
The Courtauld Gallery, London.

out to the craftsmen (who may have viewed the sample in a mirror for the purpose of constructing them)—as an exhibit these pieces may be ambiguous for the gallery visitor. The relationship between artist and craftsman was evident in the process of constructing Omega pieces but it is not clear from the exhibition who crafted the designs to fit the object, who created the charts and who made the textiles and what was the communication between artist and craftsman.

The exhibition was greatly enhanced by an illustrated pamphlet (written by Dr Caroline Levitt, visiting lecturer and associate scholar at the Courtauld Institute of Art and Joff Whitten, Education Programmes Co-ordinator, Courtauld Institute of Art) and public talks from the curatorial team as well as online podcasts presented by Dr Alexandra Gerstein (Curator for Sculpture and Decorative Arts at the Courtauld Gallery).[8] Through these we gain an insight into the relationship between the end pieces and their design process, from artist to facilitator to craftsman. Winifred Gill (who managed the workshop from 1914–16) "recalled doing a lot of rather boring routine jobs such as making the detailed charts for the carpet designs" (Levitt and Whitten 2009), thus indicating that Gill took an active part not only in the running of the workshop but in facilitating the designs for production; however the craftsmen still remain largely "unattributed" compared to the artists who have largely been "attributed" since.

One of the centerpieces of the exhibition was a rug supported by a large-scale color drawing on the wall above the piece, showing a quarter section of the rug for use by the craftsman. This is believed to have been returned to the Omega workshop by the craftsman where it was recovered in 1919. These supporting "crochets" or "charts" are crucial in the exhibition as they allow us to observe how Fry broke down the translation of ideas and aesthetics, not only to realize finished pieces but to demonstrate how he applied his philosophy to facilitate the working process from artist's hand to craftsman's delivery. By exhibiting both the "chart" and the finished piece we are able to observe the successful working relationship between Omega artists and craftsmen, indicative of the Omega's successful transition between arts and crafts (see Figures 9 and 10). The concept of buying into a lifestyle is what sells most products today and selling the genuine hand crafted one-off piece "connects the lifestyle of the artist to the purchaser." This was a strong

Figure 9
Preliminary design for Lady Hamilton Rug, Vanessa Bell, 1914. Gouache on squared paper, 419 × 803 mm (unfolded). The Courtauld Gallery, London (Samuel Courtauld Trust). Given by Pamela Diamand 1958.

selling point for the Omega artists then, as it is for designers today. The peacock stole is a good example of this (see Figure 11) supported by two drawings above its central position in the first room of the exhibition. It represents an item of clothing, personifing the influences of the avant-garde[9] and the wearer of the time. It is a statement piece more akin to a painting than a stole.

In John Ruskin's influential writings in *Unto This Last* he discusses theories on political economy and values of labor and how aspects of the imaginative life can pull on the purse strings: "Three-fourths of the demands existing in the world are romantic; founded on visions, idealisms, hopes and affections; and the regulation of the purse is, in its essence, regulation of the imagination and the heart" (Ruskin 2005: 63).

Selling the imaginative lifestyle translates to higher prices and this is what also sold the Omega workshop pieces then, in real terms and now in exhibition terms. "Its real value depends on the moral sign attached to it, just as sternly as that of a mathematical quantity depends on the algebraical sign attached to it" (Ruskin 2005: 30).

This exhibition both celebrates and contradicts Omega politics, on the one hand it exhibits the value of the one-off piece but on the other it sells Omega mass produced pieces in the Courtauld gallery shop. The "spirit" of the workshop, the carnival-like decoration of

Figure 10
Omega Workshops (Vanessa Bell), Lady Hamilton Rug. Wool, hand knotted, 184 × 92 cm. Victoria and Albert Museum, London.

the interiors (see Figure 12), which is so characteristic of the Omega experience, is not so easily translated into the gallery environment today and I feel that some of the Omega "spirit" has been lost in this translation.

However, it is interesting to note that "Omega" is the last letter in the Greek alphabet—in the late nineteenth century it was used to mean the "last word" on a subject. Could it have been Fry's vision that the Omega symbol would continue to embody his "last word" on

Figure 11
Omega Workshops, Design for Peacock Stole. Gouache and pencil on paper, 34.8 × 44.2 cm. The Courtauld Gallery, London.

Figure 12
The showroom of the Omega Workshops, July 1913, © The Samuel Courtauld Trust. The Courtauld Gallery, London.

design and philosophy on the one-off versus the mass-produced piece well into the twenty-first century?

Notes

1. A group of intellectuals, writers and artists who lived and worked in the Bloomsbury area of London at the beginning of the Twentieth century including Virginia Woolf, E. M. Forster, Roger Fry, Vanessa Bell and Duncan Grant.
2. Quoted in Gerstein (2009). Available at http://www.courtauld.ac.uk/gallery/exhibitions/2009/omega/Bloomsbury2.shtml (accessed 17/11/09)

3. John Ruskin (1819–1900) was a Victorian poet, artist, critic, social revolutionary and conservationist.

4. A member of a pacifist Christian sect founded by George Fox (d. 1691), which stresses divine influence guiding the soul and rejects sacraments and a formal ministry.

5. A movement in art, music and literature begun in Italy about 1910 and seeking to express the dynamic energy and movement of mechanical processes.

6. Dr Caroline Levitt (visiting lecturer and associate scholar at the Courtauld Institute of Art) and Joff Whitten (Education Programmes Co-ordinator, Courtauld Institute of Art).

7. A twentieth-century art movement characterized by pure and vivid color and free treatment of form.

8. For example, Gerstein, Alexandra. 2009. Podcast. http://www.courtauld.ac.uk/gallery/vodcasts/2009/bloomsbury/textiledes.shtml (accessed December 28, 2009).

9. A group of people who create or apply new ideas and techniques.

References

Gerstein, Alexandra. 2009. *Beyond Bloomsbury: Designs of the Omega Workshop 1913–19*. London: Fontanka Publishers.

Levitt, C. and Whitten, J. 2009. *Shopping at the Omega*. London: The Courtauld Gallery.

Ruskin, J. (ed.). 2005. *Unto This Last*. Lawrence, KS: Digireads.com.

Book Reviews

Book Reviews

***Kantha: The Embroidered Quilts of Bengal from the Sheldon and Jill Bonovitz Collection and the Stella Kramrisch Collection of the Philadelphia Museum of Art,* Darielle Mason (ed.), New Haven, CT: Yale University Press, 2009**

This book is a lavish publication and a wonderful example of documentation, crucially contextualizing *kantha* before time moves on and such information is lost to us. *Kantha*, the Bengali word for embroidered quilts, are here covered by six well-researched and focused essays that introduce us to the various peoples who stitched and collected them. The essays overlap each other to a degree but each has a particular focus, resulting in an outstanding book for a variety of readers, not one that is just for those interested in the textiles of India and Bangladesh or the role of women in differing cultures. The excellent illustrations throughout the book are a central part of each essay. We are given an insight into the lives, customs, religions and traditions of the people who lived and live in west Bengal and Bangladesh. Notes accompanying each essay are concise and very useful indeed.

Kantha are from the area that was once called Bengal in India. Since partition, this area now encompasses west Bengal, which remains in India, and the eastern part in Bangladesh. Like many parts of this subcontinent it has been subject to the influx of people such as the Portuguese and British who came to trade, as well as those who migrated from further west, such as the Punjab. Darielle Mason's essay places the *kantha* in Bengal with a history of the time that reminds us that when these pieces were being made this area was often in some kind of turmoil. Partition, in 1947, was not the only major event to affect this area. The movement of the capital city of India in 1911 from Calcutta (Kolkata) to Delhi had a major impact on the region, as do the frequent floods and adverse weather events that have serious effects on the lives of the people.

The period covered is from the mid-nineteenth century to the mid-twentieth century. The two collection of *kantha* housed in the Philadelphia Museum of Art form the basis of the book and this allows us to access an excellent range of examples. The Stella Kramrisch collection is shown for the first time in color, and the Jill and Sheldon Bonovitz collection is published for the first time. An introduction to these collectors is placed at the back of the book. The late Stella Kramrisch, a scholar whose work in this area was second

REVIEWED BY
ANNE MORRELL
Consultant, The Calico Museum of Textiles,
Ahmedabad, India

Textile, Volume 9, Issue 1, pp. 120–123
DOI: 10.2752/175183511X12949158771635
Reprints available directly from the Publishers.
Photocopying permitted by licence only.

to none, has her work *Kantha* (first printed in 1939) reprinted and is also portrayed in the fascinating essay by Mason. Jill and Sheldon Bonovitz are recent collectors (since 2000) and Mason not only gives us an insight into why this couple decided to collect *kantha* but also presents their views in the form of an interview.

Each *kantha* is given a separate page, making this publication a splendid resource. These beautiful pieces are now carefully cared for in the museum but they were once used domestically on a daily basis or on festive occasions. As if to emphasize the serendipitous nature of collections, a couple of the essays suggest that textiles that once were handled and used are perhaps elevated to being classed as "art" once they cross the line into being a museum piece. Some essays, particularly Katherine Hacker's, discuss the large collections of *kantha* held in museums in Calcutta and Dacca, including the collection made by Gurusaday Dutt. This inclusion is most important, as readers are informed about what is held in collections other than the two that are the focus of this book. Almost inevitably, the influence of the great Indian art historian, Ananda Coomaraswamy is felt here, as in other areas of art and craft in India.

Kantha were made from recycled old sari and dhoti cotton fabric for the layers, with the colored threads to embroider taken from the woven patterned borders. The use of this fine fabric makes for a different quality of *kantha* to those made with machine made cloth. In her essay on the technique and design Anne Peranteau describes how they are

made, the fabrics used, and the way in which stitches are used to create a variety of effects. There is an excellent description of the use of the running stitch, which is the major stitch in these pieces. The only low point is the use of Mary Thomas' *Dictionary of Embroidery Stitches* for the stitch diagrams, which are out of keeping with the way stitches are formed in this region.

The writers show how *kantha* are packed with symbols and meanings; they clearly describe how these pieces reflect religion, daily life and the use of symbolic motifs as in plants and trees, animals, birds, forms of transport from palanquin to steamer, soldiers, administrators, fertility motifs and the tree of life. Besides the images, we learn about the uses to which a *kantha* may be put, from keeping people warm to wrapping a Qur'an. The place which *kantha* take in family life, (they are handed down from generation to generation and revered as very special objects) is well understood and described. The essays provide a wonderful introduction for those not familiar with this region. The illustrations show items in use today reflected in *kantha* copying the same design or motif. Pika Ghosh discusses the relationship with other Arts and Crafts, the possible impact of woodcut prints and the link to poetry. The visual links between *kantha* and architecture are particularly apt.

Niaz Zaman discusses the issue of literacy in *kantha*. As in other areas of embroidery, the designs can be "read," or understood by people who are illiterate. They can speak to people in religious environments, much as stained glass would have done in medieval European churches. The makers of the majority of the *kantha* are not known. Nevertheless, through the text that appears, which can be in a number of languages such as Arabic, Bangla, English, Sanskrit, we may be able to gather some information as to who made it or who it was made for.

Niaz Zaman, referencing her book *The Art of Kantha Embroidery* (1981), brings to our attention the idea that a *kantha* can be a subversive textile, a woman's craft that can act as a symbol of trade, heritage or nation. Zaman tells us in the essay here how today the shift in life style, with less leisure time, means that the *kantha* is no longer in daily use. Less leisure time means any revival that is occurring is because those who find time to stitch are usually making a living from this occupation, working for craft shops or non-government organizations (NGOs). She picks up the humor that can be present too. For example, talking of the unpaid work that women carry out she says of a recent *kantha* made by Banchte Shikha, "… a woman is shown with fourteen arms, each arm performing a different job—one of which includes stitching a *kantha*—negating the statement made by many men: 'My wife does not work.'"

Book Review

Why Do Architects Wear Black?, Cordula Rau (ed.), Vienna: Springer Verlag, 2008

The debate surrounding black is far from new. The pocket-sized book *Why Do Architects Wear Black?* takes the debate to another level and asks a hundred architects "Why do architects wear black?" The book is a collection of answers from established names such as Peter Eisenman, Jacques Herzog, Rem Koolhaas, Richard Rogers, Peter Zumthor, Albert Speer and Wiel Arets. *Why Do Architects Wear Black?* does not, unfortunately, make any attempt to analyze or evaluate the answers, but merely presents the single sentence answers in the architects' own handwriting. What lies behind the dress habits of architects? What is the connection between the color black and architects? Why do architects habitually wear black? After reading the personal opinions of the selected architects the subject remains elusive and unclear.

One of the most interesting answers in the book is given by the German architect Arno Brandlhuber, who writes "They are in mourning about their many unrealized projects." Eduard François' reply is similar to his colleague, he says "Architects wear black because they are sad," though he does not explain why. The architect Albert Speer replies likewise, but more generally, "Because life is so sad." These three contributors are aware of black's origins in mourning and grief. However, as John Harvey asserts in *Men in Black*, five hundred years ago black was only worn by people in mourning or by monks, but over time the use of black underwent an interesting transformation and became a color symbolizing power: "The color of grief, of loss, of humility, of guilt, of shame has been adopted in its use by men not as the color of what they lack or have lost, but precisely as the signature of what they have: of standing, goods, mastery" (Harvey 1995: 10). Despite this metamorphosis, wearing black is often connected with death as most people still wear black for funerals.

Some of the architects expressed the opinion that black is associated with the "introverted" status of architects, giving an impression of "silent self-assurance and mystery," which helps to convey the creative power of architects. This is in fact related to the relations between non-architects and architects, some of whom see themselves as missionaries.

REVIEWED BY
AÇALYA ALLMER
Assistant Professor, Department of Architecture,
Dokuz Eylül University, Izmir, Turkey

Textile, Volume 9, Issue 1, pp. 124–125
DOI: 10.2752/175183511X12949158771671
Reprints available directly from the Publishers.
Photocopying permitted by licence only.

For several architects quoted in the book black is associated with neutrality. For example Patrick Schumacher of London replies that black is in contrast with the architecture's neutral white. Likewise Colin Fournier (London) and Lucas Young (Berlin) believe that "architects like to stay neutral so that their buildings stand out, like the way priests cherish black so that their faith stands out." The New York architect Hani Rashid believes that architects wear black in order "to disappear into space."

Among the 100 architects there are those like Meinhard von Gerkan, who touch on the issue of black's endurance as opposed to seasonal fashion colors, believing that black is eternal and timeless, as architecture should be. The French architect Dominique Perrault brings to the fore the functional side of black. He replies that black is perfect because it is possible to wear black "at a construction site, at dinner with a president, in an architecture office, in an airplane, in social and political discussions, in a night club." Oliver Toscani and Casale Marittimo believe that "it is easier to dress in black." In the German architect Stefan Behling's words, a black dress makes one "look skinny."

When we look at the answers given by the architects, a polarization becomes evident. Although some architects, such as Peter Eisenman, Peter Zumthor and Rem Koolhaas, say they do not dress in black ("I never wear black!") this is actually not the case. Some of them commenced their replies with "they," meaning that they did not include themselves among those who dress in black. In the not-so-distant-past, it was possible to tell a person's religion, rank, class or occupation from the way they dressed. However, we cannot deduce that anyone dressed entirely in black is an architect in our contemporary society. As can be seen from this book, the meanings of black are far more complex. Nevertheless, for anyone interested in the impact and importance of black in architects' choice of dress color this book is just a beginning. It is a pity that the book lacks a preface or an introduction evaluating the significance of black for architects as revealed by the answers of 100 architects.

Reference

Harvey, J. 1995. *Men in Black*. Chicago, IL: University of Chicago Press.

Book Review

Berg Encyclopedia of World Dress and Fashion, Joanne B. Eicher (ed.), Oxford: Berg, 2010

It is hard to avoid the use of superlatives in reviewing this ambitious, erudite and authoritative series. Taking dress, fashion and (implicitly) the textiles and other materials that have adorned cross-cultural bodies throughout history as its themes, this ten-volume publication (with 6,000 pages and over 2,000 images) provides an extraordinary and rigorous contribution, not only to these, but a breadth of related disciplines.

The series was the brainchild of the Editor in Chief, Joanne B. Eicher,[1] who has already made a huge contribution to these disciplines, not least in her insistence upon the use of precise and consistent terminologies that have now become standard. Each volume, co-ordinated by a specialist editor, addresses a particular region: "Africa," "Latin America and the Caribbean," "the United States and Canada," "South Asia and Southeast Asia," "Central and Southwest Asia," "East Asia," "Australia, New Zealand and the Pacific Islands," "West Europe" and "East Europe, Russia and the Caucasus." A detailed introduction to each region provides information on geography, landscape, climate and the distinguishing features of dress. The chronological spectrum dates from prehistory, whilst privileging the nineteenth to early twenty-first centuries. This is a considerable undertaking and provides invaluable context for the later periods that many readers and certainly students will consult.

Broad themes, such as technologies, globalization, occupational and religious dress are counterpoised with microsubjects such as backbone ornaments within Achuar culture and fashions influenced by the use of automobiles. Authors balance their discussions around daily appearance, the special dress of rites of passage and the exceptional. The absence of dress—nudity—is also scrutinized amongst various peoples and also in the context of age, as "unnatural" and within literary sources. At the end of each article there is a list of references and suggestions for further reading and in many instances there are cross-references to other relevant articles contained within the set.

Volume 10, "Global Perspectives," has a different format: it is divided into imaginative themes and subthemes (such

REVIEWED BY
AMY DE LA HAYE
Reader in Fashion Curation and Material Culture,
London College of Fashion

Textile, Volume 9, Issue 1, pp. 126–128
DOI: 10.2752/175183511X12949158771716
Reprints available directly from the Publishers.
Photocopying permitted by licence only.
© 2011 Berg. Printed in the United Kingdom.

as "Dress, Decorum and Interior Design," "Flowers, Fashion and the Church," "Mobile Technologies, Fashion and the Human Body" and "Cultural Authentification in Dress"). Amongst the fascinating materials-based entries that caught the attention of this fashion historical reviewer were:

- ca. 4000 BCE "Japan: Ainu make tough, lightweight, salmon-skin *chep-keri* (boots) with backward-facing fish scales for muddy and icy conditions. Orsal fin is often left in middle of sole for extra traction."
- ca. 2100 BCE "Crete: corset stiffened with copper ribs to cinch waists of men and women."
- ca. 1284 "Italy: Sequins manufacture in Venice."
- 1901 "Germany: medical literature reports that the first face-lift was performed in Berlin that year."

For the purposes of this journal, with its emphasis upon textiles, it is important to highlight the major significance accorded to textiles. Discussions of materials weave through the various narratives and there are special essays devoted to textiles. In the *South Asia and South East Asia* volume there is, for example, an essay on the sari within dress and textile history and the *East Europe, Russia, and the Caucasus* volume has a section on "Fibers and Textiles in East Europe."

Combined, the ten volumes incorporate contributions by some 600 international scholars, who were commissioned to write 760 essays and "snapshot articles." (The administration of this is a phenomenal undertaking in itself!) Their texts are accessible for the intended readership—students, general interest readers and subject specialists. Considering the tactile preoccupations of those who will consult it, the quality of the paper (the price of which has recently rocketed) is rather flimsy. The images contained within the brightly colored covers are black and white. Hard copies of the series will undoubtedly be purchased primarily by institutions (combined, the volumes cost £1,250). The encyclopedia is also available online at www.bergfashionlibrary.com, where it will be updated at least three times a year.

This impressive series has achieved its stated ambition in charting new territory and ensuring that readers "find the excitement, variety, sensuality, and complexity of dress presented in clear descriptions, reinforced by historical and cultural context."

Note

1. Joanne B. Eicher is Emeritus Regents Professor at the University of Minnesota and a worldwide authority on the anthropology of dress, with many now standard texts to her name.